CERTIFIABLY MAD

CERTIFIABLY MAD

BY "THE USUAL GANG OF IDIOTS"

FALL RIVER PRESS

New York

FALL RIVER PRESS

New York

An Imprint of Sterling Publishing
387 Park Avenue South
New York, NY 10016

Front cover art: Mark Fredrickson

ISBN 978-1-4351-4367-8

Manufactured in the United States of America

First edition
1 3 5 7 9 10 8 6 4 2

Visit MAD online at www.madmagazine.com

Though Alfred E. Neuman wasn't the first to say, "A fool and his money are soon parted,"
here's your chance to prove the old adage right—subscribe to MAD! Simply call 1-800-4-MADMAG
and mention code 5MBN2. Operators are standing by (the water cooler).

CONTENTS

Dear Roger,

Dear Roger,
Another school day is done and thnx 2 modern tech, I am now text messaging U.

IMHO, I believe "might" does not make right and the pen is mightier than the sword, which is Y I am writing U rather than simply turning U in.

I am hoping that this will open up some frank dialogue between us regarding some issues we need 2 work out.

More specifically, U stealing my homework, telling girls that I'm a hermaphrodite, and beating me up at the bike racks every day after school. :-(

Im guessing UR anger is merely an expression of some childhood trauma, and so I want 2 B understanding.

EXIT

If U wish 2 talk, I'm here 2 listen. BCOZ Roger, I care, I truly do. BCNU L8R
-Jeremy

WHOMP
BASH
HIT
TROMP
WHAM
BAFF

Myspace Dawgs,
Today I fragged Jermy the Hermy again.
-Rodge

>> If you've been spending pretty much every waking minute of every day at your computer emailing, instant messaging flaming, flirting, posting, networking, webcasting, illegally downloading and one-handed web surfing

MAD'S 50 WORST THINGS

1 >>

The one person in a billion who actually orders the "miracle" penis enlargement pills — guaranteeing we'll all continue to be bombarded with spam for them until the next 1-in-a-billion mook comes along.

Magic Meat Enhancer

2 >> Websites that spend $100 million on constant, annoying TV ads, and then fold a year later because they're $100 million in debt.

3 >> Sites that promise free searches of anyone's background, but somehow fail to tell you that it'll cost $29.99 to actually *see* the search results.

4 >> Google's tired gimmick of altering its logo depending upon the day – Lincoln's Birthday, or the opening ceremonies at the Olympics, or the discovery of lasers. Please remind us not to Google anything on the anniversary of the first treatment for anal warts.

5 >>

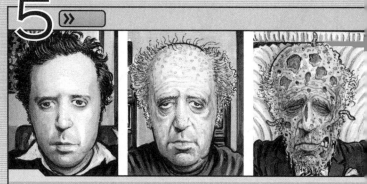

That douche-bomb who took a picture of himself every day for six years and posted it on YouTube. Hey, skippy, the only video of you we want to see is a montage of 2,190 daily shots of your occupied casket.

6 >> Online porn sites! We'll tell you the worst thing about them! It's...well...we spent hours and hours looking at them day and night, and couldn't find a single thing to complain about — except maybe that there aren't enough of them.

7 >> Not that a Google search of "George Bush sucks" gets 451,000 hits, but that "George Bush rules" gets 579,000 hits!

8 >>

SHADYCASINO.COM

Even though we can see your cards...

...we promise not to cheat!

"Gaming" websites, where the *biggest gamble* is sharing your credit card information with an offshore entity exempt from any U.S. laws, then playing games programmed by the house, which operates under no casino authority or commission rules whatsoever. Now *THAT'S* gambling!

WRITERS: CHARLIE KADAU AND JEFF KRUSE   ARTISTS: LEONARDO RODRIGUEZ

ABOUT THE INTERNET

9» Receiving the "Send this message to 10 people in the next 10 minutes and a miracle will happen!" chain emails. Unless the "miracle" is that we'll never have crap like this clog our inbox ever again, we're not interested.

10»

Online ads in which little people suddenly stroll onto your monitor screen and start gesturing and talking to you. It made us realize that if annoying, bug-sized people like this really existed in our world, we'd have no problem killing them.

11» Blogs. Who really wants to spend all their time reading the rants and musings of uninformed boors? (To read the full, extended version of this thought, visit www.myspace.com/worldofmad.)

12» Breaking News from CNN.com. When we signed up, we expected email bulletins on assassinations, natural disasters and war. Instead, we learn there's more trouble in the Hulk Hogan household, a sort-of-racy Miley Cyrus photo is in circulation, and Madonna is boffing another professional athlete.

13»

Web "celebrities" who cross over to other media. As far as we're concerned, Tila Tequila, Tay Zonday and that "Leave Britney alone" guy can all take a near-fatal leap off a platform, like that newswoman stepping on grapes did a few years back.

14» The way the hot social networking site Friendster... what? Oh, the way the hot social networking site MySpace...huh? OK, the way the hot social networking site Facebook will quickly become forgotten as yesterday's news. A friend at LinkedIn told us that.

15»

While it's easier than ever to cut and paste school papers from the web, it's also easier than ever for your teachers to *figure out* that you cut and pasted your school papers from the web.

16» Passwords. Some need six characters. Some need eight characters. Some need only letters. Some need letters AND numbers. We swear we've had to create and remember more passwords than the freakin' French Underground during all of World War II.

 17» Coming across some mutant geek emphatically arguing that the Internet and the World Wide Web aren't the same thing. They may be right, but it makes us realize that a nerd and a schmuck ARE the same thing.

 18» Parental control software like CyberPatrol and Net Nanny. Great idea: now there's *nowhere* kids can see smutty images...as long as you don't count cable TV, DVDs and the computers at their friends homes, where the parents are more realistic.

19 »

iTunes is convenient, easy to use, has a huge catalog of selections and isn't that expensive. What makes our skin crawl is every time we buy a song, we're putting 99 cents in the pocket of that pompous, mock turtleneck-wearing mega-tool Steve Jobs.

20 »

You Tube | Videos
d*ck in a box | Search

"d*ck in a box" video results 1-20 of about 2,000

| D*ck In A Box (Original) | Boobs In A Box | D*ck in a Box (Hand Puppet Remix) |

The growing number of untalented wannabes ready to pounce on a new, "hot" YouTube video with their own web-cluttering, inferior-in-every-way ripoff, reenactment or reinterpretation.

21 »

Did you see the video of the cat making a sandwich?

I also caught one with a guy's head stuck in a mini golf windmill...

How about the little girl who's a land-lord...

Saw it!

That's been up for *months!*

What are you, Amish?

The galling fact that no matter how much time you spend monitoring blogs, poring over YouTube and scouring the Web, you're never ever the first person in your circle of friends to see something on the web.

22» The harsh truth that no one, NO ONE, not a single solitary individual in all of recorded Internet history has EVER won a free iPod by correctly identifying Jessica Simpson.

23 »

You know you can't wash that without breaking it.

After winning a ferocious eBay bidding war, finding out that the description of the item you won failed to mention that it also smells like an odd combination of mothballs, curdled milk and cough syrup.

24

And another thing I can't stand about yogurt containers...

The proliferation of nonsensical podcasts and video podcasts by braindead uber-losers that make Andy Rooney's trifling whining sound like The Gettysburg Address in comparison.

25

I am King Gornad, overlord of all I survey!

The virtual world Second Life.com, which is a pretty ironic name, because just about everyone using it doesn't have a FIRST life.

26 »

E Greeting Cards — finally we have a way to show our family and friends that we care about them so little we won't even buy a cheap, 99 cent Hallmark card for them anymore.

27 »

From email to blogs to chatrooms, we now know that speeling, grammer and, punc2ation r not as improtent, as wee were taut in scool.

28 »

That AOL "You've got mail" guy – we just don't like him. In fact, now that we think about it, we really hate that sonofabitch!

29

The extra, useless sheet of paper with a single line of unneeded type on it that always seems to appear whenever you print out something from a webpage.

30 »

People on Craigslist who indicate that their personal ad includes a picture, but when the headline is clicked on, the picture turns out to be of a rainbow, or a sunset, or a kitten. Raised expectations and dashed hopes — they've just demonstrated what 99% of all online dating is like.

31 »

Illegally downloading a movie from a peer-to-peer file-sharing web site in order to save 12 bucks, and then getting sued by a movie studio for 12 *thousand* bucks. We don't know which is worse: having to pay the fine or the shame and embarrassment that comes with the whole world finding out you wanted to see *Soul Plane*.

32

Why so serious, Bats? Heehahahahee hahaha!

Netflix and Blockbuster Video's assumption that, after installing a $20,000 HD widescreen home theater system with digital surround sound and leather reclining theater seats, people would rather see a movie streamed online while hunched over a 17" computer monitor.

33

Oh, man! Todd gonna hurl!

Friends and co-workers who pressure you to watch the "Two Girls, One Cup" video, then videotape you watching it and post *that* on YouTube. Those people can go s#!$ in their hat.

34

When we just want to try a new video game demo, but first have to scroll through and "accept" terms of service agreements only slightly longer than the latest Stephen King novel. We never read them and don't know anyone who does. Hell, for all we know we may have clicked away our right to a trial by jury, signed over our pet to medical science or declared ourselves involuntary organ donors.

35

Finally putting your traumatizing high school experiences behind you, only to have them dredged up once again by those miserable Classmates.com ads.

36

When your internet browser unexpectedly shuts down, then asks if you'd like to send a report to the software manufacturer — yeah, we want Microsoft's CEO Steve Ballmer sitting home at night reading how we encountered a problem while perusing thumbnail galleries at polynesian-schoolteacher-upskirt.com

37

Ghouls whose first thought after a tragedy is, "Hey, I can use PhotoShop to come up with a funny picture!"

38

George! *Don't* turn on your computer! A *sickness* is making them *melt* — but *First* it *charges* you a *nickel* for *every* email you've *ever* sent!

Parents who can barely operate an electronic garage door opener getting on the web — and falling for every rumor and outlandish mass email they receive.

39

Online degrees. Finally, an answer to the question academics have been asking for ages: is it possible to water down the educational system even *more*?

40

That maudlin, weepy YouTube video of the guys who released their pet lion into the wild and then went to visit it a year later. We would have bookmarked it if, instead of a tearful reunion, the bloodthirsty beast went all Siegfried and Roy on them.

41

Philosophers who drone on and on about the role of the internet and what it symbolically represents in a postmodern society. Hey, Voltaire, *here's* what it represents: an easy way to order stuff tax-free, research stuff it would take months to find in a library, and look at world-class porn. Hope your ivory tower paradigm wasn't shattered by the obvious.

42 » When you accidentally roll over a banner ad that suddenly expands to totally block your screen. It reminds us of the big fat guy who always seems to sit directly in front of us at the movies, you know?

43 »

After all these years, MapQuest STILL throws in one inexplicable turn on your driving directions that has you doing a u-ey behind what looks like an uninspected meat packing plant run by guys in sunglasses and fezzes.

44 » The "personal security questions" part of registering as a user on a website. Sorry, but the name of our favorite childhood pet is none of your damn business. We still have issues surrounding Sparky's death.

45 »

Amazon's "Customers who bought this item also bought" suggestions – and its incredible accuracy at suggesting the books you *didn't* choose. It's like ordering clam chowder as an appetizer, then having the waiter suggest that you order the stuffed clams and baked clams with your meal.

46 »

Coming home and finding Chris Hanson and a *Dateline* camera crew in your kitchenette — all because the guy next door is a registered sex offender who's been trolling for 13-year-olds online by glomming on to YOUR wi-fi connection.

47 » Now that so many people rely on Wikipedia for information, the folks at Encyclopedia Britannica must be spinning in their graves — and they're not even dead. Although the Wikipedia entry on them says they are.

48 »

Perez Hilton, a bottom-feeding gossip monger who "slickly" combines John Madden Telestrator scribblings of genitalia and DNA drippings with celebrity photos, and then adds the kind of commentary previously only overheard in the bathrooms of clubs with names like "The Tranny Station."

49 » Those constant annoying reminders to update the anti-virus program. We should have guessed that their boasts about eliminating 99% of spam, pop-ups and viral annoyances would conveniently put *their* crap in the other 1%.

50 » Brainless 'tards who scoop up web domain names and hold them hostage, expecting to make millions of bucks on their sale. Screw YOU, owner of MAD.com!

It's no secret that McDonald's is trying to crawl out from under the many layers of fat that it's helped wrap around Americans. In an effort to offer a few non-lethal menu options, they now serve apples, oatmeal, and even "heart-friendly" wraps (because shoving bacon, beef, and grease into a wrap instead of a bun will add decades to your life). But we say that's not nearly enough! It's time that they Supersize their efforts and try some of these…

WAYS TO CREATE A HEALTHIER McDONALD's EXPERIENCE

WRITER AND ARTIST: TERESA BURNS PARKHURST

Like bartenders, give servers the right to refuse a customer who's had too much.

Decrease the size of a large soda to something a little smaller than a baby pool.

Include McDiabetes blood sugar tests in Happy Meals.

With a hint of laxative per serving, and strategically placed restrooms, it may be possible to *lose* a Quarter Pounder at McDonald's.

Let the Golden Arches reveal some statistic that really matters to the consumer.

Add (way) more mirrors to the décor.

Make McNuggets in the shape of fruits and vegetables so kids can at least start to identify them.

Have the self-serve ketchup area be more of a Nautilus experience.

Close the damn drive-thru window.

Now that all of the next-generation video game systems have been released, you're probably up to your eyeballs in eerily-realistic sword-swinging, zombie-blasting, Nazi-killing madness. Sure, the Xbox 360, PS3 and Nintendo Wii are okay, but you're probably getting fed up with these totally...

UNEXPECTED HASSLES OF NEW VIDEO GAME CONSOLES

GAMEPRO NINTENDO WII SUCKS!

The inevitability that, once the dust settles, one of the new consoles will be regarded as the "crappy one" — and you have a bad feeling that it'll probably be yours.

COME ON, WE'RE LEAVING FOR GRANDMA'S!

I DON'T WANT TO GO!

WE BUY YOU THAT XBOX, AND THIS IS HOW YOU THANK US?

Your cheapskate parents act as if finally buying you something cool entitles them to lord it over you like extortionist loan sharks.

I GOT WINNER!

C'MON! I'M PLAYING NEXT!

BUT, GUYS, IT'S MY GAME... WHEN DO I GET TO PLAY?

Your TV room will suddenly be filled with more dubious new "friends" than a trailer-trash PowerBall winner.

BLAM!

BAM!

IF I'D KNOWN THIS WAS COMING, I COULDA SAVED MYSELF TEN BUCKS!

The new consoles' power allows for new heights of plotting and character development in the latest *Tomb Raider*, *Resident Evil* and *Doom* games — making you wonder why the same couldn't have been done for those awful movies.

WRITER: JACOB LAMBERT   ARTIST: PETER BAGGE

In order to afford the system, the endless peripherals and the latest games, you'll have to work so much that you can barely even play the freakin' thing.

The amazing combination of team play, passing skills and tough defense in the new crop of NBA games will make it even tougher to stomach the sloppy real thing.

Wireless controllers just give your sore-loser friends one more easily-chucked object to wing at your head.

Incredible graphics make even the dullest games seem cool — at least until you actually play

The new consoles consolidate mp3, DVD, and the Internet into one place — which will also be the site of vicious family battles over who gets to use it.

Taking out the trash, feeding the fish, making sure your crusty undies make it to the hamper — it's how kids earn a living. But responsibilities, like smel

WHAT I GOTTA DO

for my ALLOWANCE!

As everybody in the universe knows, J.K. Rowling's wizard story comes in seven parts. In the first book, Voldemort tries to kill Harry. In the second book, Voldemort tries to kill Harry. In the third, Rowling shakes up the formula in a major way: Voldemort's HELPER tries to kill Harry. Book #4? Zap, we're right back to Voldemort trying to kill Harry. And now it's time for the big-screen version of Book #5. Although we don't want to give away any of the surprises, let's just say that a certain Mr. V has some nasty plans for our hero. Come ON, already! We're dying to see SOMEthing, ANYTHING, that's even a little bit different! But this drip-drip-drip formula is just...

The **buzz** is that **this** is the **darkest installment** of the **Harry Plodder** series **to date!**

Yeah, yeah. The **darkest one yet!** The **darkest one yet!** The **movie company** promotes EVERY sequel as "the **darkest one yet**"! Number **seven** will probably be an **all-black screen!**

Hear ye! Hear ye! The **trial** of **Harry Plodder** is now in **session!** You stand accused of **growing up** so **uncute** that even **pedophiles** no longer **download** your **photos!**

You stand accused of **possessing** just **two acting techniques**: either standing around in **open-mouthed astonishment**, or **petulant outbursts** of **anger!**

You stand accused of taking **seven books** to get to the **ending** of a so-called **saga** that could have been **knocked off** in **two!** Three, tops!

You stand accused of relying on **bogus suspense**, like whether or not you'll get **killed** in the **fifth book** of a **seven-book series**, or how this trial's **verdict** will turn out in the **first 15 minutes** of a two-hour movie!

And you stand accused of being a powerful **wizard**, world-famous **celebrity** and superstar **athlete** who STILL can't **figure out** how to **get a date!** Harry Plodder, how do you **plead?** Other than in a flat, uninvolving **monotone?**

Poor Harry! Up against a **handpicked panel** of cruel, arbitrary, unsympathetic **British judges!**

I'll say they are! They **rejected ME** for being **too much** of a creampuff!

THE JUDGE IS IN

MARRIAGE LICENSE

Plodder AND THE TORTURE OF THE FANBASE

WRITER: DESMOND DEVLIN   **ARTIST: TOM RICHMOND**

I **don't!** I'll just **wait around** for a random **plot twist** to show up, just like I **always** do! Glowing **unicorn**, valiant **phoenix**, parents' **ghosts**, **time travel**...Good ol' **J.K.** always pulls some cheap, outlandish **surprise** out of her **butt**, at exactly the **critical moment**, just to **save my bacon!**

Yoo hoo! Did I hear "**random plot twist**"? My **spectral essence** has arrived to **clear** Harry of **all charges!** Let us **remember** the legal **precept** of *habeus corpus*! As well as *amicus curae*! And especially *non sequitur*, because this **trial scene** makes absolutely **no sense!** But most of all, *Fergalicious!* My **body** stay **vicious**, I be up in the **gym** workin' on my **fitness!** *Ipso facto, a fortiori*, and in **conclusion**, let me say that if the **Sorting Hat** doesn't **fit**, you must **acquit!** I'd also like to enter my **beard** as "**Exhibit B**," for no special reason!

Ahhh, I should've **listened** to the **showbiz adage**: "Never work with **dragons** or **children!**" But I'm **Lord Druckermort!** I'll end up **on top!** Right **now**, though, I'm in a strange **limbo**, stuck **halfway** between **life** and **death**. Much like Lindsay Lohan's **career!**

We gave our **lives** to **protect** our **baby Harry**, and keep him **safe** from **harm!** Since then, he's only been attacked by giant **spiders**, murderous living **trees**, bone-chilling **soul-suckers**, evil **elves**, a three-headed **watchdog**, underwater **shrimp-warriors**, fire-breathing **dragons**, a crazed **werewolf**, a gigantic poisonous **snake**, and the most diabolical **wizard** ever! Um...**mission accomplished?**

Harry wishes we were still **alive** and could be **with** him **every moment** of **every day!** Which makes him the **opposite** of **every kid** sitting in this **movie theater!**

I REALLY ♥ HORSES

21

Haggard's gone and they've replaced him with a centaur! Professor McConjugal was attacked and sent to the hospital! Doubledork has disappeared!

The Queasy twins have just quit school! Druckermort has almost captured the ultimate weapon!

Everything's happening too fast!

Hey, YOU try cramming 869 pages of book into a lousy two-hour movie! That whole subplot about Haggard's giant half-brother Grawp can only be glimpsed briefly in the reflection of my eyeglasses!

Brrr! Another nightmare about Seriously Wacked being tortured by Druckermort in a room of spheres! I've got to contact Seriously somehow! Should I use the two-way magic mirror that's right next to my bed? Nah! Instead, I think I'll try breaking and entering into the private office of my #1 enemy at Halfwits! It's foolproof! And I'm just the fool who'll prove it!

Harry's picking up Seriously Wacked's trail like a homing pigeon, and he's making a beeline for the Ministry! He's got to stop Druckermort the snake from killing Seriously the dog! And we're coming along, like a bunch of prize jackasses!

I can feel it! We need to walk down THIS hallway! Just like in my snake dream!

You didn't happen to dream the location of the loo, did you? Because all this suspense has my bladder ready to blow!

CAUTION! UNEXPECTED SURPRISE ATTACK AHEAD

APPROACHING SECRET DOOR!

Yikes! Five of Lord Druckermort's personal Death Eaters!

Actually, I'm more of a Death Snacker! Eating Death always goes right to my hips!

Come one step closer, and I'll smash it! I'll destroy the crucial sphere!

The prophecy contained in that sphere reveals how we will kill you! So tell us how we'll kill you, or else we'll kill you!

Why couldn't you just pick up the sphere and read it yourself?

Oh, NOW you're asking for logic in these stories? If Druckermort could visit the inside of your head and read your thoughts, why did he wait four years to do it? If we needed you to enter the sphere room for us, so that we wouldn't get caught breaking into the Ministry, why did we just break in anyway? Why could you go back in time to restore the life of a stupid eagle-horse two movies ago, but anyone killed in this movie has to stay dead? THINK, Plodder! Without arbitrary plot devices, you'd have been snuffed in your crib!

One Fine Day on Main Street

WRITER: MICHAEL GALLAGHER   ARTIST: PAUL COKER

What School Bus Drivers are Doing While You're in Class!

MESSING WITH THE WINDOWS

HAVING FLEA MARKETS WITH ALL THE STUFF KIDS LEAVE BEHIND

FINALLY AIRING OUT THAT NASTY CASE OF ASSNE

BLASTING ALL THE DIESEL-FUMEY SNOTS OUT OF THEIR NOSES

WRITER AND ARTIST: TERESA BURNS PARKHURST

Is this another installment of Al Jaffee's popular, long-running feature? Why yes, yes it is

SNAPPY ANSWERS

WRITER AND ARTIST: AL JAFFEE

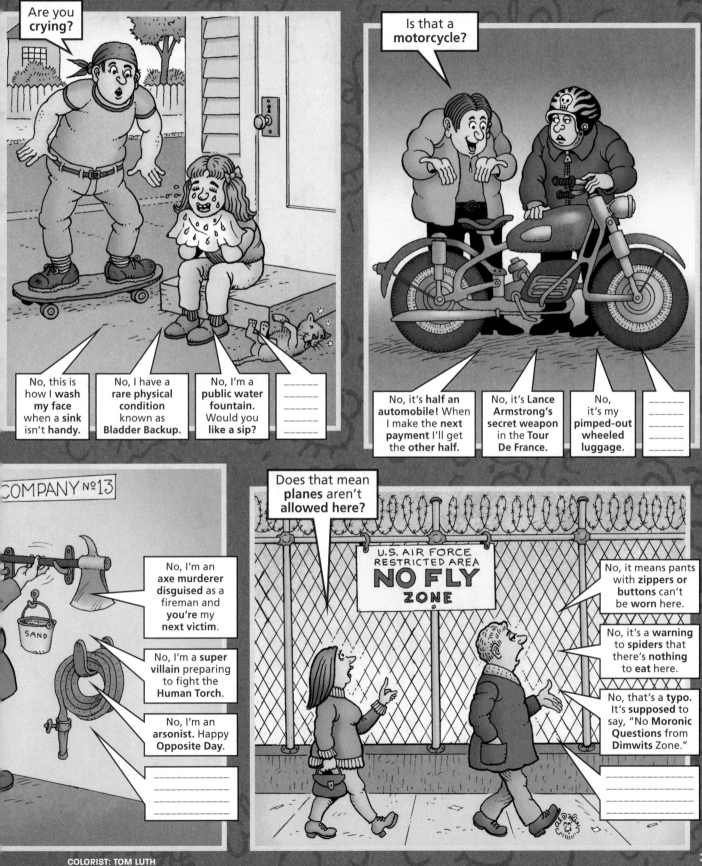

Sergio Aragonés Presents A MAD Look

WRITER AND ARTIST: SERGIO ARAGONÉS   COLORIST: TOM LUTH

THE DISSING LINK DEPT.

The game "Six Degrees of Kevin Bacon" is extremely difficult — not because it's hard to connect people, but because people don't know who Kevin Bacon is anymore! But we here at MAD won't let a little thing like "staying current" get in the way of presenting you with yet another installment...

6 DEGREES OF SEPARATION

Can you connect CORPORATE SCANDALS to HILARY DUFF CDs?

Corporate Scandals — require the manipulation of numbers, as does... **Sudoku** — which is a serious drain on people's time, as is... **Instant Messaging**

Can you connect THE FLAG-BURNING AMENDMENT to MEL GIBSON?

The Flag-Burning Amendment — has miraculously managed not to die, just like... **Bob Barker** — who shepherds annoying schlubs on and off stage, just like... **American Idol**

Can you connect DRUGS to LIVING IN IRAQ?

Drugs — are a self-destructive habit, as is... **Hunting with Dick Cheney** — which is a perk for GOP contributors, like... **No-Bid Government Contracts** — HALLIBURTON

Can you connect THE BOY SCOUTS to MELISSA RIVERS?

The Boy Scouts — provide a role model for American youth, as does... **Cartman** — HEY YOU BITCH ASS! — who's a big-headed cartoon character, as is... **Terrell Owens**

WRITER: MIKE SNID

BETWEENANYONEANDANYTHING PART IX

Viewing One Night in Paris on the Internet

Which can produce Carpal Tunnel Syndrome, as can...

Oscar the Grouch

which is dirty and mostly green, as is...

Hilary Duff CDs

who spends most of his time in a garbage pail, much like...

Scientology

which is devotedly followed by mindless millions, as is...

The Anti-Immigration Lobby

which blames aliens for all of our troubles, as does...

Mel Gibson

which is hurtful to minorities, as is...

"Hillary in 2008" Signs

which get Democrats all worked up," as do...

Bird Flu

which will soon be everywhere, like...

Living in Iraq

which has a 50% mortality rate, as does...

Brokeback Mountain

who makes old-time cowboy-fans cringe, as does...

MAD Kids

which spawned lots of bad jokes last year, as did...

Melissa Rivers

which is a junior version of an awful original, as is...

Some people are blessed with skin as soft and smooth as the freshly driven snow. They always look good in photos, always have a date on Friday night, and always seem to come out on top in life. We hate these people. Then there are others, like Jeff in the purchasing department. Hoo-Boy! To call this guy Pizza Face would be an insult to pizza! Jeff could eat a vat of Proactiv and it wouldn't do any good. What about your skin? Have you looked in the mirror lately? Are you like Jeff?

ARE YOU A CANDIDATE FOR THE ZIT HALL OF FAME?

Has popping one of your pimples frequently resulted in a severe case of whiplash?

Are you able to drastically reduce your body weight with just one pimple popping session?

WRITER AND ARTIST: TOM CHENEY
COLORIST: CARL PETERSON

Has the ineffectiveness of
acne medication forced you to
switch to power tools instead?

Have you ever used your complexion
as a means of self defense?

Does your skin condition interfere
with your use of sporting equipment?

Do your blemishes sometimes erupt
unexpectedly during changes
in aircraft cabin pressure?

Can popping your larger pimples
result in property damage?

Have you ever had to wear a "zit bra"
to keep your larger blemishes
from jiggling while you walk?

Have your pimples ever been the direct cause
of an embarrassing tattooing accident?

Are your pimples large enough
to get caught in things?

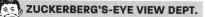

Aside from Snooki and Justin Bieber, there are few things in modern life that are as unavoidable as Facebook. Unlike Snooks and Beebs, though, Facebook is great for lots of things: connecting with friends, sharing photos, and posting real-time updates on your love of Jujubes. But these benefits are far outweighed by the many, many things that flat-out suck about the site — beginning with...

THE 50 WORST THINGS ABOUT facebook

1 Facebook has 500 million users and is valued at 65 billion dollars — which means that your membership alone has put $130 in the pocket of Mark Zuckerberg's faded, smelly hoodie.

2 The fact that the first response to just about every new Facebook setting or feature is, "How do I opt out of this?"

3 Knowing that the 70 people who wrote "Happy Bday!" on your wall didn't actually remember your birthday, but just saw the notification.

 Mark
Happy 35th Birthday!

Kim
happy 37th big guy

Zach
The big 3–0!

Josh
Dude I thought you died

4 The unbelievably clever practice of purposely misspelling your name in your profile to elude college admissions officers and potential employers — go feck yourselves.

5 The devil and angel that appear on your shoulders as you debate whether to accept or ignore your grandmother's friend request.

6 When you post a trivial political viewpoint, and someone who disagrees with you replies with a point-by-point manifesto so long it would make the Unabomber drowsy.

 Ryan
I just read an article in USA Today that says the deficit actually went DOWN last year.

 Michelle
Ok...first off, the article makes an erroneous assumption that the budget was set in the first four months. The historic stimulus bill added 200 billion to the deficit in 2009, and that's just one of the spending items on Obama's shopping list, according to figures from the CBO...
See more. Much, much more

7 The knowledge that no matter what your privacy settings are, any creep, lunatic or pervert could be looking at your profile picture *right now*.

MMMMM -- CANCUN ALBUM! JACKPOT!

8 The growing segment of the population that always talks about Facebook, even when they're NOT logged on to Facebook.

SO MY FRIEND FRANK'S STATUS IS "GO JETS," AND THEN I CLICK THAT I LIKE IT, BUT THEN IN THE COMMENTS I SAY, "YOU MEAN AT THE AIRPORT, RIGHT? BECAUSE THE TEAM SUCKS! LOL!"

9 Facebook chat — it cuts out and logs off at a rate that makes us nostalgic for AOL 2.0.

10 The bland and pointless info section, where your boring answers to insipid categories like "interests" and "activities" make this month's Playmate sound like Shakespeare in comparison.

11 Friends inviting you to view albums of parties you weren't invited to.

THERE'S ANN, AND ROB, AND SCOTTY, AND JENN...THE ALBUM IS CALLED "PARTY LAST WEEKEND"...WHAT THE...?!?

12 The charming way your boyfriend changed his status from "in a relationship" to "single" a full three hours before calling to inform you of this development.

13 Friends who hijack your profile and make subtle, clever changes...like incorporating the word "poop" into your current status.

14 Tagging yourself as your "celebrity doppelganger" — congratulations! You've reaffirmed what everyone on the planet already knew: 1) You're an egomaniac and 2) You don't look an effin' THING like Adrian Grenier.

15 The never-ending, narcissistic quest for the perfect new profile picture.

A SHOT OF ME AND THAT SUNSET WOULD BE PERFECT FOR MY PROFILE PIC!

BUT MY WATER JUST BROKE!

SCENIC VIEW

16 People who show support for a cause by changing their status update for an hour — after which they can go right back to not really giving a damn.

17 The fact that Facebook's business model is built entirely on sucking away your every last molecule of privacy so they can hawk it to advertisers.

Jacob
RIP Grandma Rose. You will be in my heart always

Brooks Brothers
Jacob! Save 30% on funeral wear at Brooks Brothers!

18 Facebook's penchant for constant profile overhauls and redesigns that improve upon the original almost as much as that time Heinz decided to make blue ketchup.

19 Getting excited about 12 notifications, only to discover that 10 of them contain the word "zombie."

20
Facebook "Friend suggestions" that are as clueless and awful as Amazon's book recommendations.

HMMM... FACEBOOK THINKS I WANT TO BE FRIENDS WITH MY EX AND THE BITCH HE LEFT ME FOR!

21
"Liking" — we just don't like it.

22
Companies that beg you to "Friend us on Facebook" — because you've always dreamt of getting hourly updates from Stubbins Pest Control.

23
Your parents on Facebook.

Karen
At dinner with the girls ;-)

Karen's Mom
Remember shellfish gives you gas!

24
Pictures that girls take of themselves with the same seductive head tilt that, because of how they have to hold the camera, show mostly armpit.

25
Having your account hacked into so it looks like you're shilling products.

Charlie
I did not send the message "I'm having such great results with Enhanz-Plus All-Natural Male Enhancement Pills," or that they "make my man-quarters feel like a steam locomotive of explosive sex-passion" – my account was hacked into! Please believe me!

Joe
LOL! Awesome, dude – you are the KING! Choo-choo! All aboard!

26
Friend requests from estranged camp bunkmates, third cousins, former landlords, that guy you were in a car accident with and other dregs from your life that you hoped you'd never hear from again.

27
"Never-Ending Quizzes" that are somehow more addictive than meth, yet a hundred times less productive.

28
The Bermuda Triangle-esque vortex of time-wasting, where you sign in just to check your latest updates, and suddenly it's eight hours later and you've seen every picture taken of your friends since they were 12.

HUH. I DIDN'T KNOW JEFF PLAYED PEE-WEE SOCCER.

29
Pathetically forcing yourself to invite those strange semi-friends from high school back into your life just to buff up your anemic friend count.

30
TMI statuses.

Ben
Status: Stomach bug finally gone! Soooo much diarrhea!

31

People who don't realize just how morbid it is to "Like" a status that begins with "RIP."

Andy
RIP Michael Jackson.
👍 53 People Like This.

Bridget
Nice status!

Jesse
super like. RIP

32
People who have been on Facebook for a solid two years and are STILL using that creepy "silhouette" default profile pic.

33
The depressing realization that, if Bigfoot does exist, he would be on Facebook now, too. But, since he's not, case finally closed.

34
"Zany," warped, Photo Booth profile pictures. Actually, the "twirl" function *does* make you look a little less cross-eyed.

35
Trying to explain to your mail-order transgender illegal immigrant life partner why your relationship status is "It's complicated" without hurting his/her feelings.

36
Douches who not only regale you with updates of what they've just eaten, but also upload pictures of the meal — as if you otherwise wouldn't believe the existence of a ham and cheddar omelet.

37
Reunions that never would have happened without Facebook's help putting everyone in touch — and that, once you're at them, make you realize why they never should have happened.

38
Tagging all of your friends in those little cartoon spreads with side-splitting aliases like "the drama queen" and "the ladies man," because the only thing better than being friends with you is having your personality reduced to a three-word cliché.

39
People who smugly brag that they're "not on Facebook" — which is just as well, since, beyond that fascinating factoid, they have absolutely NOTHING to share.

40
Back-and-forth Facebook "conversations" that, unlike real conversations, rapidly devolve into lazy, one-word grunts.

Doug
Hey, how'd it go today? I know you were nervous about it.

Trevor
It went great, thanks. It wasn't that bad after all.

Doug
That's good.

Trevor
Yeah.

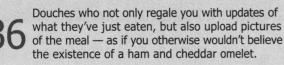
Doug
ok

41 The sad, inescapable truth that the amount of Facebook "poking" you do is inversely proportionate to the amount you do in real life.

42 Facebook's regular, unannounced altering of privacy settings — which are slightly less difficult to undo than cracking the DaVinci Code.

43 The lack of a "Dislike" feature.

44 When the only people who "Like" your shirtless beefcake pics of yourself are close relatives.

Brad
Spring Break Photos 2011

Brad's Aunt
Very handsome!!!

45 Getting fired because some a-hole took the time to tag you in the far corner of a party photo taking a bong hit.

46 The surprising success of *The Social Network* — which means it won't be long until we see movies based on the thrilling creation of Google, Mapquest, and GoDaddy.com.

47 The unsettling realization that whenever you try to delete your profile, Facebook goes all HAL on you.

48 Event invitations: Great! Mark your calendars for "I dropped my phone in the toilet and now I need everybody's numbers" and "If enough people join this group I'll shave my eyebrows"!

49 Facebook Mobile — because what's **really** been missing from the Facebook experience are blurry uploaded cell phone pics and car accidents resulting from you updating your status.

50 The haunting realization that when you get right down to it, Facebook is a thorough, complete and undying record of every stupid thing you've ever done.

47

Horror fans! There's nothing scarier than watching our society be destroyed by a snarling mob of vicious, unreasoning, soulless cannibals with no thought besides a furious hunger without end, and no goal beyond devouring their fellow man. But until the Republican and Democratic conventions start up, you'll just have to make do with...

THE WALK

Imagine a **fearsome world** where people **drop like flies**, every minute could be the **end**, and the survivors **envy** those who are **gone**. But enough about **series creator Frank Darabont** and the **original writing staff**! I'm **Officer Stain Warped**, and I'm the **last living member** of Georgia's police department. I was a **lumpy loser** until my partner **Thick Grunts** was presumably **killed**, and I got to become his **wife's lover**. I'm telling you, this **deadly zombie virus** is better than **eHarmony**! As Thick's **most trusted friend**, I always had my **partner's back**! And the **same** goes for his **widow**. I had **her back**. And her **front**, too!

Just to be **clear** — it's **not cheating** if you have **sex** with your **husband's best friend** while your **husband** is **comatose**. Although it's **polite** to move him **out of the bed first**! What can I say? I **go** for a **man in uniform**. I once **slept** with the **entire day shift** at **Chuck E. Cheese**. But **don't** judge me for **what I did**, and who I did, and in **how many positions**. I'd been given **false information** that my **husband** was **dead**! That's when I went through the classic **five stages** of grief: denial, **anger, depression, horniness** and **infection**!

I'm her kid, **Kid**! This has been a **confusing time** for me. I have all the **natural, normal fears** of any kid adjusting to a **second father**. Can I **love him** as much? Should I call him **Daddy**? And will my **real dad** come back and **eat my face**

I'm **Merde**. I **hate Arabs, beaners, chinks, dagos**, and **all other minorities**! I may be a **repulsive racist**, but I'm **alphabetically organized**! This outbreak finally gave me a **Z** to add to my list of hate: **zombies**! If that **ethnic-looking** one over there **bites me**, I'll catch his **zombie virus**, but he'll get **five diseases** back from **me**!

I'm **Merde's** redneck brother, **Feral Dickweed**! I'm **more civilized** and **genteel** than my big brother. That just means that **unlike** him, I hired a **tattoo** *professional* to **engrave** the **swastika** on my **genitals**! The group needs an **expert hunter** like me. With my **crossbow**, I can hit a deer **right between the eyes** from a **thousand feet**! You should have heard the kids at the petting zoo **crying**! Buncha **pansies**!

What a choice! Leave our **campground** and risk sudden, violent **death**! Or **stay here** with these two **ignorant, bigoted rednecks** and maybe end up **hanging** from a **tree**! I just hope I don't choose **wrong**! None of this seems **real**. Watching my comrades fight **zombies** is like living inside a **video game**. Except **our** personalities aren't as **emotionally complex** and **nuanced** as **Kirby** or **Wario**!

As the **elder** of the group, the others look to **me** for my **time-tested wisdom**. In other words, I'm the **neighborhood coot!** I watched a pack of **zombies** bite their way through my **wife's intestines!** Figures! She hadn't given **ME** a **hot meal** in **twenty years!** Seeing them eat her alive has **motivated** me. I'm going to **fight** to **survive** as long as it takes for my **prostate** to **harden**. If I gotta **go**, at **least** I want to give one of those **bastards** a **stomachache!**

One way to **stop** a **zombie** is to **smash its head** with a **baseball bat**, really **hard**, with **strength** and **ability!** That explains why the **Seattle Mariners** were the **first to die!** My **outdoor skills** have gotten me this far. If we're going to live through this, we've got to **scavenge**. **Food**, yes. **Weapons**, sure. All the **used-up clichés** from all the **other zombie stories?** Most **definitely!**

Take it from me, no matter **how frustrated** you get, **never** tell a **zombie** "Hey pal, **bite me!**"

Society has **collapsed**, and we're all **total strangers** who've somehow **banded together**. For once, one of these corny **MAD intros** with everyone **standing around** awkwardly and **introducing** themselves makes **narrative sense!** My name is **Anemia**, and I try to remain **philosophical** about our **terrible situation**. Sometimes it takes a **crisis** before you find out **what** you're **made of**. Unfortunately, **another** way to find out is **after** they **chew you open!**

I don't really **fit in** with a **post-apocalyptic meltdown** in which every spark of **humanity** has been utterly **crushed** and **spiritual survival** is an **impossibility**. I bring the mood **down!** I wasn't **always** this **depressed**, though. I used to be **worse! I used** to work on the **shrinking staff** of a major **city newspaper**. Finally I feel like I've got a **new lease on life!**

See what you **miss** by being in a **coma** for a month? The **world** I knew is **gone**, my own **family** thinks I'm **dead**, and I have absolutely no idea **who** got **eliminated** on *So You Think You Can Dance!* I'm **Thick Grunts**, and I've learned a **lot** in the past **48 hours**. The **city** is **completely overrun** with **murderous zombies**. But I have a **plan**. I'm going to go from the **city** to the **suburbs**, then back to the **city**, then to the **woods**, then back to the **city**, then back to the **woods**, then back to the **city!** That's all I got. But at least if the zombies **eat my brain**, they'll **die of starvation!**

WRITER: DESMOND DEVLIN   ARTIST: HERMANN MEJIA

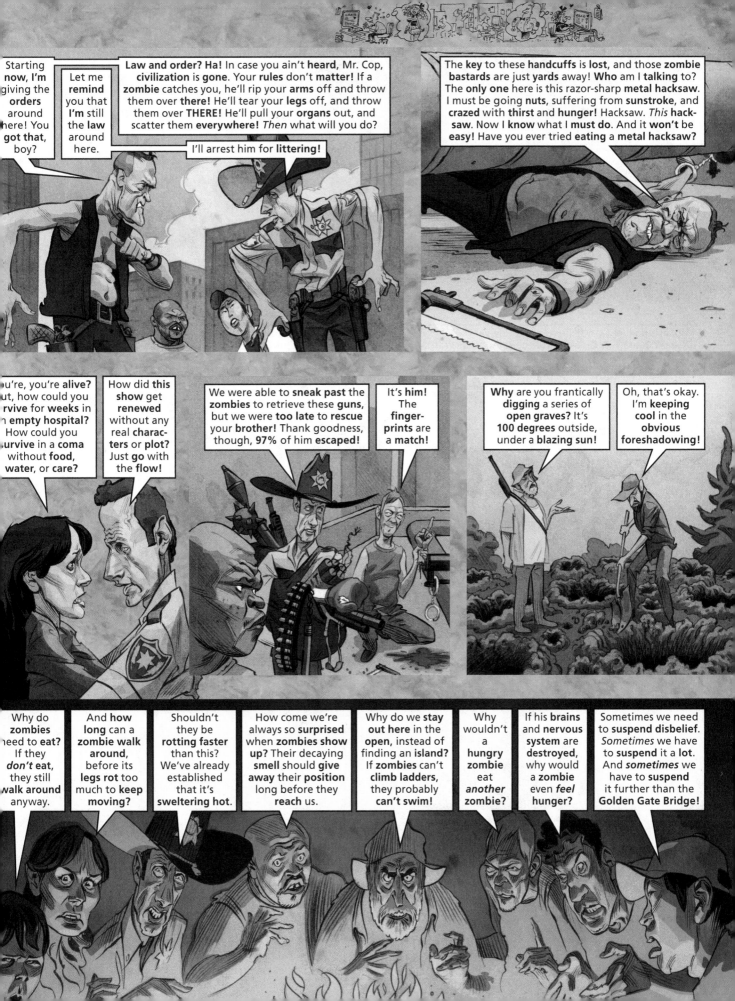

OTHER RULES

INSPIRED BY THE

5 SECOND RULE

Everybody knows the 5-Second Rule: after you drop a piece of food on the floor, you've got 5 seconds to pick it up before it officially becomes "dirty" and not edible. It's one of those rules that helps people live their lives (and contract salmonella). But some need more help than others (especially MAD readers)! And that's why we've come up with these…

10-Second Rule

How long you can hold you wife's purse before it becomes emasculating.

7-Second Rule

How long you can stand in front of an ATM looking at your receipt before the guy behind you makes a comment.

2-Second Rule

How long you may "shake" at the urinal before zipping up and flushing.

4-Second Rule

How long you can safely stare at your friend's girl-friend's boobs before getting punched in the face.

3-Second Rule

How long you have to wait after someone relinquishes the "best TV seat" before you're allowed to scramble over and take it.

:01 :03 :05

14-Second Rule

How long you have to pin on your prom date's corsage before her parents suspect you're trying to cop a cheap feel.

35-Second Rule

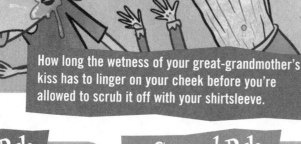

How long the wetness of your great-grandmother's kiss has to linger on your cheek before you're allowed to scrub it off with your shirtsleeve.

420-Second Rule

How long you can be in a locked bathroom before your mom asks, "What are you doing in there?"

29-Second Rule

How long you have to mourn your dead goldfish before you flush him.

11-Second Rule

How long you can let a dog sniff your crotch before the owner thinks you're enjoying it.

RITER: JOHN SAMONY   ARTIST: JOSE GARIBALDI

6-Second Rule

How long you have to wait after asking "Who wants the last doughnut?" before you're allowed to snatch up the last doughnut.

14-Second Rule

How long you can make silly faces at a little kid in the grocery store before his parents start to feel a little uncomfortable.

49-Second Rule

How long you can sniff your T-shirts to determine if you can get one more day out of them before taking your roommate's advice to "just wash them already."

25-Second Rule

How long you have to wait after your teacher walks by before you can go back to texting.

9-Second Rule

How long you can ogle the *Hustler* and *Barely Legal* covers at a magazine stand before the other customers think you're a perv.

.0005-Second Rule

How long you can read a MAD article before you get sick of the same old tired jokes.

BOOK CLUB

Fan-Favorite Sequels!

Harry Potter and the Half-Blood Prince

J.K. Rowling   652 pages
Own the latest Harry Potter adventure — even though all your friends already read and discussed it long ago. Perfect for students whose parents were too lame to let them stay up to buy it right at midnight when it first came out!

Pay More $!

~~$19.95~~   **$21.50**

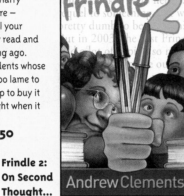

Andrew Clements

NEW!

Frindle 2: On Second Thought...

Andrew Clements   250 pages
In fifth grade, clever troublemaker Nick Allen asked why a pen needed to be called a pen — why couldn't it be called a...Frindle? Before he knew it, his crazy experiment had become a national phenomenon and everyone was calling pens "Frindles." In this satisfactory sequel, Nick decides that maybe "Pen" was a better name after all and that whole "Frindle" stuff was just a stupid waste of time. As the book ends, a pen is no longer a Frindle — it's a pen!

$7.95

Good Enough!

Falling Up the Light Sidewalk Where the Attic Ends

Shel Silverstein   184 pages
This brand new book features never-before-seen poems from the late Shel Silverstein. Of course, they've never been seen before because they're all awful and were cut from his aweful books. Collected from his old garbage can!

$19.98   ~~$18.98~~

Falling Up the Light Sidewalk Where the Attic Ends

Shel Silverstein

Most Pages Are Numbered!

Holes 2: Fill 'Er Up!

Louis Sachar   262 pages
Jonathan Nahtanoj's luck has run out! He's been sentenced to Camp Green Lake for a crime he didn't commit. The warden has a new punishment to help the young inmates "develop character" — namely, filling in all the holes she had them dig in the first book, so that sod can be laid down. You'll learn important lessons about friendship, integrity and landscaping.

$11.35

Great for Burning!

The Panic

K.A. Applegate

Animorphs: The Panic

K.A. Applegate   202 pages
When the Yeerk aliens threaten to launch a massive attack that threatens everyone on the planet, how will the Animorphs stop them? Probably by morphing into animals, right? **$4.95**

The Princess Diaries: Prom Princess!

MEG CABOT

The Princess Diaries: Prom Princess!

By Meg Cabot   306 pages
Mia Thermopolis went from an awkward teenager to the princess of Genovia! And now this princess wants to be queen... prom queen, that is! But, after a failed attempt at a coup, will she have enough time to find the perfect dress AND execute the coup's conspirators and their families?

$16.99

IF YOU LOVE HARRY POTTER, THEN YOU'LL KIND OF LIKE THESE KNOCK-OFFS!

THE MAGICAL KEY

The Magical Key

Hector Spackle   285 pages
Marvin's dad has a magical key that could lead to amazing powers — or just unlock that linen closet! Even after finishing the book, it won't be clear. First book in a series of 20!

$7.95

All Sales Final!

The Cheetah, the Wizard, and the Bureau

4 Books — 1 High Price!

The Chronicles of Narnia Fantasy Grab Bag

Want *The Lion, the Witch, and the Wardrobe*? Well, if you do, you also have to take 3 other vaguely-related books that you'd never buy any other way! Comes with *The Cheetah, the Wizard, and the Bureau*, *Magicfire: The Curse of Troll Grove* and *Zelborn Revisted — Book the Third: The Saga of Norzibeth* — all magically forgettable!

$42.50

The Fourth Summer of the Sisterhood

Ann Brashares   402 pages
Lena, Bridget, Carmen and Tibby are back — and so are their traveling pants! Join them as they embark on adventures of love, life and the Laundromat — to finally wash those filthy, reeking pants they've been sharing for the last three years. It's about time!

~~$7.95~~   **$8.95**

WRITER: DAVE CROATTO   ARTISTS: SCOTT BRICHER AND GARY HALLGREN

HISTORY COMES ALIVE
BY BEING SLIGHTLY LESS BORING THAN SCHOOL!

The Great American Journey

Meg Chunder   304 pages

Felicity and Abigail are leaving their home in Richmond, Virginia to explore the wild frontiers of America! Will these courageous cousins survive the long, lonely trip to California and the many obstacles they'll face along the way? Things are looking pretty good, since they're flying business class on a 747!

$10.95 $9.95

M E G   C H U N D E R
THE GREAT AMERICAN JOURNEY

The Complete History of the World

Marshall Phlegm   48 pages

From the Big Bang to cavemen to the 1967 World Series to today, learn what happened during all 13.7 billion years! 48 exciting pages — plus stickers!

$2.95

Miranda Hudge: Freedom Fighter

Tiffany Flump   215 pages

Read this amazing true story about a girl just like you! Well except that she spent her childhood freeing slaves, fighting censorship and working with the Queen — while you pretty much go straight home and eat Doritos in front of the TV!

$11.95

Miranda Hudge: Freedom Fighter
By Tiffany Flump

The Holocaust.

Jeremy McDeedles   126 pages

The shocking and heartbreaking story of the systematic execution of over 6 million Jews, homosexuals, gypsies and other minorities. A grave and important tale for young readers to learn — as told from the perspective of "Strudel," Hitler's mischievous pet beagle! From the author of *Patches & Mandela — The Schnauzer That Helped End Apartheid!*

$9.95

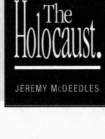

The Holocaust.
JEREMY McDEEDLES

Wheels of Change

Franklin Tubbings   ??? pages

Clara is the first black student at Hawkings Middle School — and everyone's angry! Except for Belle, who wants to be friends with the new girl — until she decides it's just too much of a hassle. But will Belle's new lemonade stand raise enough money to get her that new bike? Only time will tell!

$2.95

Wheels of Change
FRANKLIN TUBBINGS

The Castle's Secret

R. I. P. Deadingham   207 pages

A mysterious couple is keeping Riley prisoner! Can his best friend Charlie uncover the secret of the Castle of Mirrors to save him? Yes, he can. Sorry if that ruined the ending... but you'll still buy it, right?

$6.59 $7.50

The Castle's Secret
By R. I. P. Deadingham

Sci-Fi, Fantasy, Thrillers and Who-Cares-Who-Dun-Its!

Inkspot by

Cornelia Funke   650 pages

Meggie's father, Mo, has the ability to bring characters to life, just by reading about them! While reading a story to baby Meggie, he brought the book's villains into his world — and accidentally banished Meggie's mother to theirs! Now, with no wife and a better understanding of his special powers, the thrilling series' conclusion finds Mo reading aloud from *Penthouse Forum*. What started as a tragic story concludes with multiple happy endings!

$17.95

CORNELIA FUNKE
INKSPOT

On the Run: Road Ragers

Gordon Korman   160 pages

Aiden and May Falconer's parents are facing life in prison for a crime they didn't commit. With their parents trapped in jail with no way out, Aiden and May secretly travel the country with just one mission in mind — to have the coolest, most fun-filled roadtrip ever! It's non-stop fun from New York to San Francisco with no parents, no bedtimes, no curfews and no rules!

$4.99

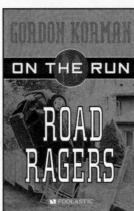

GORDON KORMAN
ON THE RUN
ROAD RAGERS
FOOLASTIC

"A Summer to...Remember?"

J.B. Spookington   185 pages

Lily has amnesia and can't remember she's the reason her hamster died 10 years ago — even worse, she's just moved to a new town and suspects the her neighbors may be vampires! Can Lily endure the Civil Rights tensions of 1964 — and her first real crush! — during a summer she won't soon forget?

$7.95

"A Summer to... Remember?"
FOOLASTIC
J.B. SPOOKINGTON

FOOLASTIC BOOK CLUB

Zoey 101: School Daze
112 pages
Read this hilarious new adventure, based on the hit TV show that your parents yelled at you for watching too much — which is what started them nagging you to read more to begin with!

$2.95

No Good!

No Longer Printed with Toxic Ink!

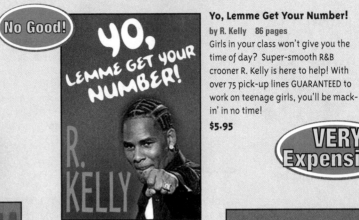

Yo, Lemme Get Your Number!
by R. Kelly   86 pages
Girls in your class won't give you the time of day? Super-smooth R&B crooner R. Kelly is here to help! With over 75 pick-up lines GUARANTEED to work on teenage girls, you'll be mackin' in no time!

$5.95

VERY Expensive!

Sudoku
Check out the ancient Japanese number game that's sweeping the country! 43 puzzles requiring intense concentration and problem-solving skills! It's like having extra math homework that you do just for fun!

SUDOKU OVER 40 PUZZLES!

Perfect for Nerds!

$5.95 ~~$4.50~~

Guaranteed Highest Price!

What a Load of Craft!
Learn calligraphy, knitting, pottery and more!
Wendy O'Bendy   112 pages
Now you can MAKE birthday and holiday gifts for all your friends — and you can take all the money you would have spent on them and just spend it on yourself! Like on more books! Right...?

$14.95

what a load of craft!

Learn calligraphy, knitting, pottery and more!

Hilary Duff: When the Going Gets Duff, the Duff Gets Going
Jerome McTatertot   18 pages
She's one of the hottest stars alive! But what's she really like? What was her life like before she got famous? What makes Hilary tick? These questions and many more won't be answered by this 18-page booklet of trivia you already knew and photos from back when she was still on *Lizzie McGuire*! But it's glossy!

$3.25

Hilary Duff
When the Going Gets Duff, the Duff Gets Going!

Rejected for a Caldecott Medal!

MAD Libs!
A Series of Uneventful Misfortunes
48 pages
If you love the adventures of the Baudelaire Orphans, now you can write your own silly adventures. Pick the name of a new guardian for the orphans, a new alias for Count Olaf and a new town name and you're done! Come to think of it, it's not like Lemony Snicket does much more than that in each book anyway...

$1.95

A Series of Uneventful Misfortunes
MAD LIBS
A super silly way to fill in the _____!

Lame!

Personal Organizer and Spellchecker
Requires 7 D Batteries
Now you can organize your assignments, mark down important test dates, even check the grammar and spelling on your homework. The perfect tool to help you in your studies! At least that's what you'll tell your parents — they don't need to know that you only want it because you can also play "Hangman" on it!

$12.95

NEW!

101 Jokes, Riddles and Puns That Will Leave You Baffled
Boyd Will B. Boyd   38 pages
"How many unicorns does it take to screw in a lightbulb? Eight... nine if it's a Wednesday!" "What do a flashlight and a sub-stitute teacher have in common? They both love a *leap* year!" Plus 99 other weird jokes that make no sense! From the Creators of *101 Poorly-Translated Foreign Jokes*

$5.50 ~~$4.25~~

101 JOKES, RIDDLES AND PUNS THAT WILL LEAVE YOU BAFFLED!

VRRR

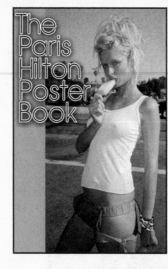

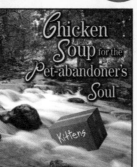

It's been four long, sad years since that grossmeister John Caldwell wrote another "Gross and Beyond Gross" article. That is, the years have been long and sad for John — we've rather enjoyed the break! But all good things must come to an end, that's why we reluctantly give you...

JOHN CALDWELL's FINAL INSTALLMENT OF THE

GROSS AND BEYOND GROSS
TRILOGY

GROSS IS...

...Following a night of partying, you suddenly realize that the toothbrush you're using is not your own.

BEYOND GROSS IS...

...Following a night of partying, you suddenly realize that the toothbrush you're using is not really a toothbrush.

GROSS IS...

Scuzzy restaurant kitchen help who ignore the "Employees Must Wash Hands After Using Restroom" sign.

BEYOND GROSS IS...

Scuzzy restaurant kitchen help who never bother to *use* the restroom.

WRITER AND ARTIST: JOHN CALDWELL

GROSS IS...

...Downing a mouthful of your favorite snack only to discover it has an expired freshness date on the label.

BEYOND GROSS IS...

...Downing a mouthful of your favorite snack only to discover it has an expired field mouse in the bag.

GROSS IS...

...People who wear painful looking, ostentatious nose piercings that you can't help but notice.

BEYOND GROSS IS...

...People who wear painful looking, ostentatious nose piercings that you never notice due to the size of the hanging booger.

GROSS IS...

...Finding evidence in the front seat that your mechanic smoked in your car.

BEYOND GROSS IS...

People who plan their dinner *menu* around watching *Fear Factor*.

BEYOND GROSS IS...

...Finding evidence in the back seat as to why he needed a cigarette.

SERGIO ARAGONÉS PRESENTS A MAD LOOK AT

WRITER AND ARTIST: SERGIO ARAGONÉS

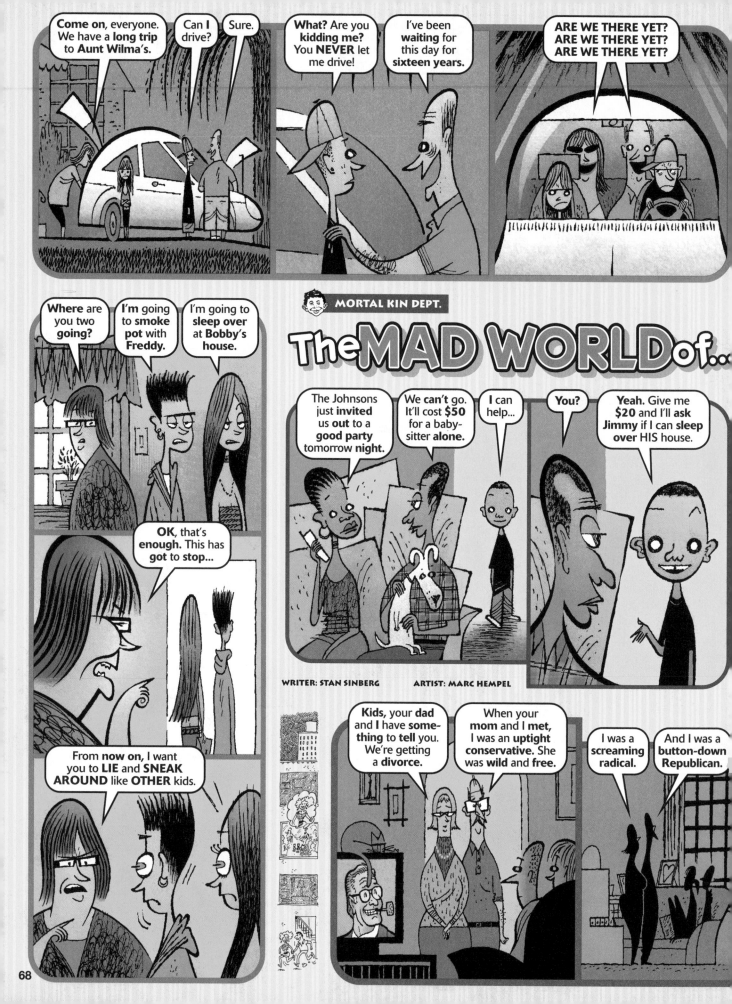

FAMILY LIFE

Recently, MAD was approached with an exciting offer from a major publishing house. They offered us the chance to print excerpts from whichever of two books we preferred: either 2006 Nobel Prize-winning chemist Roger D. Kornberg's advanced treatise on eukaryotic transcription at the molecular level, or singing sensation Justin Bieber's autobiography. Naturally, the staff was torn. But since we'd already scheduled "Sergio Aragonés Looks at Cytoplasmic Mitochondria" to run in MAD #509, for this issue we're going to go with...

100% SUPERFICIAL
JUSTIN BIEBER
First Step 2 Obscurity: My Story

Lots of photos for your locker or prison wall

Love, Justin's Ghostwriter
xoxo

*"I need somebody,
I, I need somebody.
I need somebody,
I, I need somebody.
I need somebody,
I, I need somebody.
I need somebody,
I, I need somebody."*
—Justin Bieber,
"Somebody to Love"

I'll never forget writing those lyrics. Through the verbal medium of words, I was trying to capture the feeling of needing somebody. Did I accomplish my goal? Yes I did. Although I'll always wonder if maybe I should have stuck in one more "I need somebody" just to make sure my message shone through.

These are the questions that torment my music and provide its depth. But I guess creative restlessness is crucial to my being the great songwriter that I am.

And I couldn't do it without you, the fans. That song is about you. All of you are that somebody I need. And without everybody being my special somebody, I'd be nobody. Just ask anybody.

Therefore, I dedicate this book to you. I value my relationship with you so much. It's so valuable, I could never, ever put a pricetag on it. However, I do know that California residents must add 8.25% sales tax.

Luv Ya, Justin

WRITER: DESMOND DEVLIN   ARTIST: SCOTT BRICHER

I know what the haters are thinking. Most celebrity autobiographies are vanity press ego trips. You might be worried that this book will be a big, fat valentine to myself. Not to worry, I'm Canadian. And we don't celebrate Valentine's Day in Canada. We don't, right? Or maybe I'm thinking of Labor Day.

And yes, I've heard the old joke about the celebrity author who's written more books than he's read. In my case, that's not true. I've read *The Very Hungry Caterpillar* AND *The Grouchy Ladybug*, even the scary parts. And I'm almost halfway through *Goodnight Gorilla.*

Despite my literary credentials, people have asked me how I can have the egotistical gall to release the story of my life when I'm just 16 years old. Well, what about Anne Frank? She was only 15, and nobody complains that she put out her autobiography. Anyway, she seems a little overrated. If she was SUCH a great author, why didn't she ever write a second book?

What's the secret behind the Bieber Cut? My hair wasn't always this perfect, until one day I got cornered in the bathroom by a bully, who turned me upside-down and gave me a toilet bowl swirly. I cried a lot that day. But then my hair dried like this and the rest is history. I suppose I should really thank that bully. But I'm still a little nervous. Hey, she was the second-biggest girl in class.

Now I'm a great author, but my #1 job will always be putting out R&B songs for people who are a little intimidated by the music on *Glee.* However, you can't make everything totally vanilla. You have to show the world that you have an edge. And we all know I'm a rulebreaker!!! Like this one time, a few months ago, I was doing a signing appearance. And at the end, I pocketed the Sharpie. Hey, don't cross this wildcat's path — you might get scratched!

I know how fortunate I am. I don't know what an economy is, but I do know this is a rough one. That's why I made a special trip to Michigan to do a free concert for the unemployed steelworkers. Times are hard for them, but I knew they would appreciate seeing a 16-year-old multimillionaire.

I felt my amazing success was just the thing to lift the community's spirits. Like there was this one guy, Jerry. He's 48 years old and suddenly his entire way of life is gone, poof, and it's never coming back. Medical coverage, mortgage payments, his children's future, and he's lost it all. The least I can do is dance around and sing "Eenie Meenie."

And I think Jerry appreciated it. He gave me one of the very last exhaust systems that he built before they cut his job and shut down the factory. He probably should have brought it backstage, instead of chucking it off the balcony. If it had landed two feet closer, I wouldn't be writing this now, ha, ha! But I guess Jerry probably doesn't get to go to a lot of concerts and doesn't know the etiquette.

My fans say that I sing like a bird. Unfortunately, I also have the depth perception of a bird. At least when it comes to glass doors. They're my Lex Luthor. I must have smacked my face into glass doors on all ten continents. Why do you think my lips are the size of two swimming pool floaties? Oh well, it's good for my pores.

Actually, I walk into a lot of solid doors, too. It's just that most of those collisions never get posted on YouTube. It's much harder to film me through solid doors.

Phew! I never knew writing a book would be this hard! Each page is like a million tweets! Of course, Twitter is hard, too. I never have enough thinking in my head to fill up the message. Thanks, exclamation points!!

I guess this would be a good spot to list the rest of my exclusive Twitter Tips:

"Sooooooo" fills more space than "so." It's the perfect word to use when your message is sooooooo vapid!

Every concert should always be described as "crazy." Awards are also "crazy." The tour is "crazy." Photo shoots are "crazy." Basketball is "crazy." Meeting celebrities is "crazy." But using a thesaurus would be insane.

Condense your text by using numbers in every message; for example, "2 awesome!" or "b4" or "some1." Less commonly, you may get to use "4closure," "circumnavig8," or "9, Mein Fuhrer!"

It's no wonder I have millions of followers who can't wait to hear what my typing finger thinks. In fact, I was the number one Twitter trend of the year. Suck it, Haiti earthquake!!!

Two years ago, I was an unknown with 4 or 5 online clips that my mom put up. Today, there are over one million Bieber videos on YouTube. And fewer than half of those claim I've just been killed by a speeding car, a terrorist bomb, electrocution, getting mauled by a moose, or all four. I was really sad when I saw those clips, until my manager told me they were hoaxes.

But just like my voice, I haven't changed. I'm still me. I'm still the same wide-eyed kid who used to sing for coins on the streets of Ontario. It's just that now, I have six huge NFL guys on injured reserve to keep away the grabbers and the slobs, a small army of Teamsters who set up the equipment every night for my epic 12-second drum solo, and my own line of cosmetics. I'm very proud of those. It's just like rubbing me onto your face!

The awkward pratfalls. The audience of little kids. The haircut. What can I say? The man is my role model!

Not only am I a legendary recording artist and an important author, but I'm also a movie star! After being in the public eye since mid-2009, it was time for me to branch out. My movie is called *Never Say Never*, and I'll be playing an innocuous pretty boy singer from Canada who hits it big singing bland pop songs for the girlies. I just hope I can figure out how to play the part! I'm talking to the director about possibly dyeing my eyebrows, because I'd love to take this story to some unexpected places.

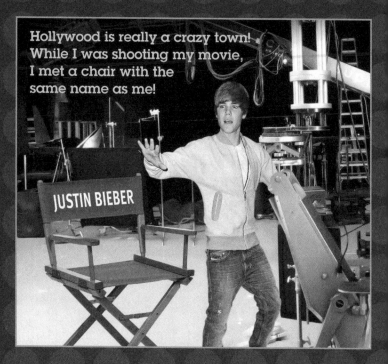

Hollywood is really a crazy town! While I was shooting my movie, I met a chair with the same name as me!

JUSTIN BIEBER

We're going to be releasing *Never Say Never* in 3-D, so if you thought my lips were puffy before, wait till you strap in! Some people say that 3-D is just a lame fad. But that's what they said about my singing career, and I'm still here! It just goes to show that true quality always lasts.

SPOILER ALERT: I'm adorable!

Next week, we film my new video. I haven't seen the shooting schedule yet, but I'm going to go out on a limb and guess it's about a shawty who stares into my eyes for three minutes. Then, at the end, she succumbs to her wild animal passions and touches my shoulders. Hey, even my fans have to learn about s-e-x sometime.

It's true that we use average-looking girls in my videos. It's part of the Bieber Master Plan. Rule One: nobody's allowed to be cuter than me. Ever. Also, it lets all my dopey fans imagine that if I'm making my googly love face at some charity case, they could get me, too. I'm always telling my fans to believe in dreams. So if you're a civilian and you think that someday you might be my girlfriend...keep dreaming!

For my videos, I insist on doing my own choreography. Sometimes I point into the camera, but other times I point up in the air. Sometimes I hold my arms apart, but other times I touch my chest. I even clutched my fists once, but that reflected a dark side of me I don't like to acknowledge. For next year, I'm thinking seriously about adding an actual dance step!

The Nick Kids Choice Awards was off the hook. I got slimed. It was so gross! The next day, I read a review of the show that said, "Watching that cold, disgusting green slime ooze down into Bieber's ears was the perfect metaphor for the rest of us, who have to endure hearing his odious, abhorrent music."

Whoa! Thanks, dude! You called me "perfect"!

This is me pointing, from my "Baby" video. The next one is me pointing from "One Time." Then it's me pointing from "Never Say Never." And you know I had to do a little pointing in "One Less Lonely Girl." What surprises will the future bring? I'm a bit of a chameleon, so I'm not sure myself!

Wow, are we at the end of my first book already? It's amazing how fast 240 pages can fly by, although the 217 color photos didn't hurt.

I'm soooooo glad you took a trip into my world. I hope that my autobiography proves to have even more timeless literary value than the Situation's, or the one by that Miss USA beauty pageant loser who didn't want the gays to get married.

I promise you, this amazing journey has only just started. And I'm inspired by something a great man once said: "Pick it up, pick it up. Pick it up, pick it up. Up, up up, up up, up, up."

Hey, wait a second! That great man was me!

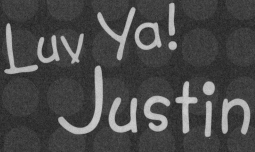

ONE DAY AT LINCOLN HIGH

WRITER AND ARTIST: ERIC SCOTT

MAD's Helpful Guide to
-The Chronicles of-
Narnia
Prince Caspian

The first *Chronicles of Narnia* film was a $750 million blockbuster. And now the Lion and the Witch are both back! (The Wardrobe held out for more money and the producers cut his part.) But what if you're among those who didn't see the first movie? Is the complex fantasy world of Narnia and all its characters too detailed to keep straight? Worry no more! For those of you who can't tell a Spiderwick from a Dementor because you made the mistake of not being an escapist geek, just bring this article with you to the cineplex!

WRITER: DESMOND DEVLIN
ARTIST: HERMANN MEJIA

*T*he *Chronicles Of Narnia: Prince Caspian* is the sequel to 2005's *The Chronicles of Narnia: The Lion, the Witch and the Wardrobe*, the saga which has been called "a timeless classic" by hundreds of people who work in the acquisitions and promotions departments at Walt Disney Pictures. It is based on the much-loved books by C.S. Lewis which, thanks to the existence of these movies, need never be read again.

Prince Caspian is the second big-screen chapter in what is projected to be a seven-movie series. *The Chronicles of Narnia: The Voyage of the Dawn Treader* will be next. Some possible titles for future installments include:

⚜ *The Chronicles of Narnia: Special Victims Unit*

⚜ *The Chronicles of Narnia: The Zesty Guardians of Stoobletown*

⚜ *The Chronicles of Narnia: The Divine Secrets of the Ya-Ya Sisterhood*

⚜ *The Chronicles of Narnia: Back in the Habit*

⚜ *The Chronicles of Narnia: Enter the Man-Pumpkin*

⚜ *Tyler Perry's The Chronicles of Narnia*

⚜ *The Chronicles of Narnia: The Glue Gun of Vengeance*

⚜ *The Chronicles of Narnia: The Search for Spock*

⚜ *The Chronicles of Narnia: Christmas with the Kranks*

⚜ *The Chronicles of Narnia: Narnier Than Ever!*

NARNIA (pronounced MID∗dil Erth) is a magical realm of mythical creatures who live in natural harmony amid the gently rolling hills that encircle the divine river, and who, once in a while, will shoot you in the face with arrows. It's also an inconvenient commute. Narnia can only be reached by passing through magical portals. Fortunately enough, magical portals just so happen to follow the Pevensie kids everywhere they go, like mall security.

Azkaban

Allowance wasteland

Familiar territory

non-CGI props

danger! here be critics!

The MAD map of NARNIA

kingdom of tie-ins

tolkienswipe

Kingdom
of the
Crystal Skull

east
gobbledygook

merchandising stream

sea
of
endless
hype

ye olde
codpiece shoppe

poorly-rendered
forest

point of
confusion

jesusfreak creek

tomb of the
unknown cast

bridge to
terabithia/
nim's island

unwanted
sequel
path

trumpkin towers

starbucks

Camelot

MAP WRITER: JACOB LAMBERT

Aslan the talking lion is a lion who talks. He possesses the ultimate power to change anything. This is incredibly handy every fifteen or twenty minutes, whenever the story crashes into a dead end. Aslan has complete knowledge of deep magic, deeper magic, and magic so deeply deep you'd need a shovel to dig it up. As a lion who can do his own tricks, he's like a one-stop Siegfried and Roy show, without the two creepy Germans.

Many readers see Aslan as a substitute Christ figure, since he dies for the sins of others and is later resurrected. There is also a current eBay auction for a waffle with Aslan's face on it. If true, the *Narnia* films are just the latest Hollywood hits to feature hidden, subliminal references to Christianity, following such movies as *E.T.* and *The Passion of the Christ*.

Aslan is always wise, compassionate and beloved, not counting the part in the first film when he ripped the White Witch's intestines out with his claws and teeth. The role of Aslan originally belonged to Jack Black, but he was replaced by a CGI character when the moviemakers decided Black was too hairy to believably play a lion.

Prince Caspian is the rightful heir to the kingdom, but he has to flee Narnia for his life. In exile, he rallies his supporters and prepares to defeat King Miraz in war, with the help of interdimensional allies, last-second divine intervention and a talking badger. It's pretty much the same victory plan that Bush has for Iraq.

At the end of the story, he's crowned Caspian X. (Spoiler Alert: he's not a Black Muslim.) King Caspian is not sure that he's worthy of the throne. Supposedly his own opinion of himself is because he's so modest and humble. But let's look at Caspian's glorious résumé. He runs away in the night like a yellow dog, he doesn't look where he's going and gets whonked in the head by a tree, he has his unconscious butt saved by two dwarfs, and then he summons some little kids to fight his battle for him.

"Possibly not worthy"? "Modest and humble"? Yeah, right. "Knows full well he sucks harder than a Eureka Upright Vacuum Cleaner" is more like it.

King Miraz may as well be wearing a baseball cap with the words "BAD GUY" on the front. Miraz became king by killing his brother and usurping his throne, then plotting to remove his Danish nephew, Hamlet... er, we mean, Prince Caspian. Apparently in Narnia the plagiarism laws are loosely enforced.

Miraz attempts to wipe out all existing traces of Old Narnia's history, but his Wikipedia-style edit war is unsuccessful. So he leads his army halfway across Narnia before inexplicably agreeing to fight a one-on-one, winner-takes-all duel. For a kingdom he already rules. Slick move. Miraz may have been wearing his gold crown two sizes too tight.

The Pevensie Children—
Peter, Susan, Edmund and L[ucy]

are the main heroes of the saga. All four Pevens[ies]
strong wills, good hearts and totally great hair.

Peter Pevensie, the oldest, has the pleasantly bla[nk]
looks of a *Sims* avatar, but not the acting range.

Susan proves her mettle by tirelessly lugging her [bow through]
the unforgiving Narnia terrain.

The stumblebum Edmund almost died in the fi[rst movie]
twice. But he manages to win his greatest triu[mph to]
date in *Prince Caspian*, when he just barely out-w[its]
a dwarf. Give the guy another four or five movi[es and]
eventually, Edmund may work his way up to bei[ng able]
to dribble a basketball one-handed.

Lucy carries a "healing cordial," and just one dro[p can]
bring someone back from death's door. It is Lucy'[s abid-]
ing belief that guides the children through perilo[us times,]
though it's a lot easier to be brave when you're t[he]
one carrying a jug of magically convenient get-w[ell juice.]

At the end of the story, Aslan tells Peter and Sus[an, who are]
14 and 13 years old respectively, that they will n[ever be]
allowed back to Narnia again because they're no[w too old.]
That's Hollywood for you!

Reepicheep

is that rarest of
Disney-related characters: a
mouse who actually does something.
He valiantly leads a squadron of 12
warrior mice against the enemy, where
they run around and stab the soldiers'
feet. After Reepicheep's tail is cut off
in the fight, Aslan the lion uses his
omnipotent energy to restore it. For
an all-powerful godhead, Aslan is a bit
of a micromanager.

Dwarfs are native to Narnia, and come in two v[arieties: nice]
and kind Red Dwarfs, and the more malevolent [Black Dwarfs.]
They are distinguished by the color of their hair, [but, to be]
100% certain, it's always a good idea to check th[at the carpet]
matches the drapes. Other mystical inhabitants [of Narnia]
include Gnomes, Ogres, Mermen, Centaurs, Drag[ons, Sea]
Serpents, Unicorns and Presbyterians.

Trumpkin the Dwarf

is captured by Mi[raz's]
soldiers, who transport him all the way to the [sea]
to be murdered. Because it's not as if they coul[d just stay]
home and drown a dwarf in the sink. After Trum[pkin is]
rescued by the Pevensies, he tells them about th[e good old]
days in Narnia. It's the most touching movie sce[ne involving]
a nostalgic dwarf since Billy Crystal reminisced a[bout Yankee]
Stadium in *City Slickers*. The Pevensie children g[row fond of]
Trumpkin, and give him the nickname "D.L.F.," w[hich stands]
for "Dear Little Friend." This acronym is not to b[e confused]
with "D.I.L.F.," which stands for something else [entirely.]

MAD's Bewitching PRINCE CASPIAN Outtakes

Do I hear the song "It's a Small World After All"? Wow, those Disney self-promotion hacks think of everything!

Now why did I come into the forest? Good lord, after 1,300 years I'm having a senior moment!

Before I kill you, would you mind helping me find the thumb I just cut off...?

Is that a Lacoste logo?

WAY OUT

I bet the audiences wish they had a sign like that...

Sigh...Peter's been standing there for hours. He just doesn't understand that there are no escalators here.

It's good...that you just got the new issue of MAD Magazine. It's better...that you have some free time to read through it. But it totally sucks...that it's filled with lame-o garbage like...

IT'S GOOD...
...BUT IT TO

It's GOOD...

When you get your highest score ever on *Grand Theft Auto*.

...It's BETTER...

When you get to taunt the friend you beat about it.

...But it TOTALLY SUCKS...

When he responds by acting out a scene from the game — on your face!

It's GOOD...

When your folks get you a cell phone.

...It's BETTER...

When they give you unlimited minutes.

...But it TOTALLY SUCKS...

WHO ARE YOU WITH? WALK THE DOG! WHAT TIME WILL YOU BE HOME? NO! NO! NO! BUY MILK! WHERE ARE YOU? DID YOU EAT?

That they call every 5 minutes checking up on you!

It's GOOD...

When you make the football team.

...It's BETTER...

When you're named starting quarterback.

...But it TOTALLY SUCKS...

If your offensive line is the worst in the league!

IT'S BETTER... TALLY SUCKS...

It's GOOD...

When your parents let you camp out all night for Kanye West tickets.

...It's BETTER...

When you're first in line.

...But it TOTALLY SUCKS...

When scalpers STILL manage to bribe their way to all the good tickets!

It's GOOD...

When you wake up to discover that it snowed last night.

...It's BETTER...

When they cancel school.

...But it TOTALLY SUCKS...

That you're forced to spend most of your day off helping your father shovel out the driveway!

It's GOOD...

When you finally finish setting up your MySpace page.

...It's BETTER...

When, on the first day, you already have dozens of friends.

...But it TOTALLY SUCKS...

When all of those "friends" turn out to be middle-aged sex offenders who will probably wind up on *Dateline*!

WRITER: DAVID SHAYNE   ARTIST: RICK TULKA

85

There's a show on MTV that's all about spoiled, obnoxious, selfish douche bags. No, not *Laguna Beach*. Or *The Real World*. Or *Maui Fever*. Or *24/7 Party People*. Actually, we probably should've been more specific — this show focuses on 16th birthday parties. And if there was ever a bunch that truly deserved some birthday punches, it's the "stars" of...

My Stupid SPOILED 16

It's **my party** and **money** is **no object!** Mostly because it's not *my* money...

That's **right** — it's **Erica's birthday** and whatever she **wants**, she **gets!**

Ugh! This show is like the **Make a Wish Foundation** for hateful little **bitches!**

I **need** to get a **rap star** to perform at **my party.**

That's **really expensive**, honey — that's going to cost **tens of thousands of dollars!**

I don't **care!** People at my school are **expecting** it — I'll be an **outcast!** They'll **never** speak to me **again!**

Here's an **idea** — instead of trying to win them over with a **big concert**, how about I just give **every person** in your school **200 bucks** to be your friend?

WRITER: DAVE CROATTO   ARTIST: HERMANN MEJIA

Listen up — I'm going to be **handing out** my **invitations**, so **pay attention!**

Wouldn't *mailing* your invitations be an **easier** way to let people know they're **invited?**

Duh! The whole **point** is to let people know they're **NOT invited!** And **this** way, everyone can see how **hurt** and **embarrassed** those **losers** are! **Ohhh** — zoom in on **that girl** I didn't invite — she was my **lab partner** and she thinks we're **friends!** Ha ha ha!

Look at this — rolling up in a **Bentley, swarmed** by **photographers**, everyone screaming my **name** — I'm a **celebrity!**

Are you **retarded?** You **rented** a luxury car, **hired** photographers, and **invited** all these **people** to come to a party that **YOU** threw for **YOURSELF!** That's like **hiring two prostitutes**, then **bragging** about having a **threesome!**

For decades, the Walt Disney company has been churning out cheery cartoons where everything works out right, the hero learns an important lesson, and everyone lives happily ever after. Meanwhile, back here in reality, the bad guys often win, history inevitably repeats itself and the good guy doesn't always get the girl. So, the next time you find yourself being brainwashed by Disney's heartwarming treacle, take a moment to have a reality check and consider...

What to Disney in the

Aladdin would be detained indefinitely at Guantanamo Bay

Pocahontas would work as a blackjack dealer at an Indian reservation casino

Captain Hook would never get past an airport security checkpoint

WRITER: ADAM RUST   ARTIST: DREW FRIEDMAN

Would Happen Characters Real World?

Three years after being smuggled into the country in the cargo hold of a decrepit freighter, Mulan would become the multi-millionaire owner of a chain of nail salons

Donald Duck would contract bird flu from Daisy

Bambi's fur, a haven for ticks, would give Lyme disease to hikers and campers all along the Eastern seaboard

Mary Poppins would have to compete with Filipino women for nanny gigs

Tragically, Jiminy Cricket would get eaten by the Geico gecko

Belle would get the *Queer Eye* guys to give Beast a makeover

The Seven Dwarfs would be unemployed victims of corporate downsizing and outsourcing

95

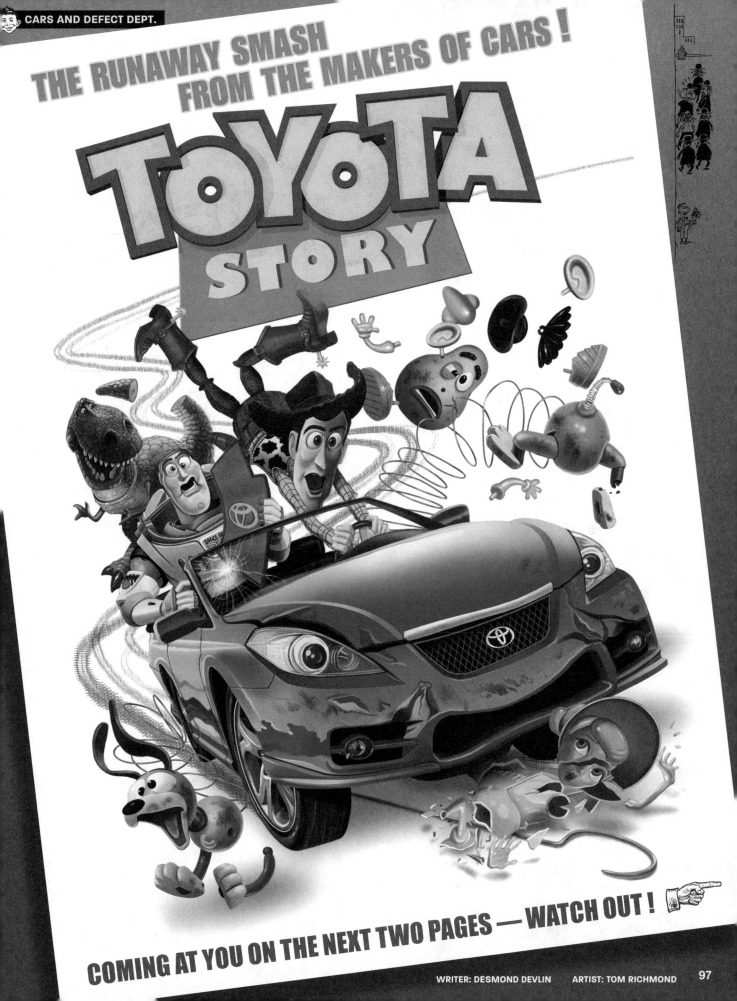

THE RUNAWAY SMASH FROM THE MAKERS OF CARS!

TOYOTA STORY

COMING AT YOU ON THE NEXT TWO PAGES — WATCH OUT!

WRITER: DESMOND DEVLIN   ARTIST: TOM RICHMOND

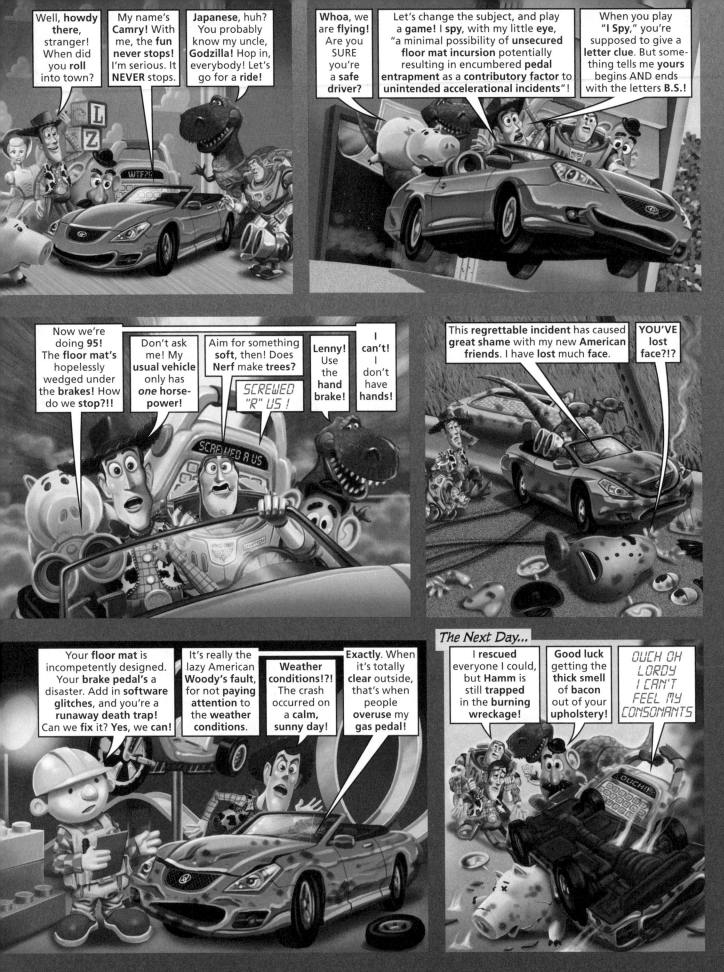

The savage forces of evil are on the rise! They plan to crush the wizard world! Their dark reign of terror is on the verge of succeeding! And what's got our dweeby hero worried? See, there's this girl that he just realized he likes, only she likes another boy, kind of, but it's complicated because she's the sister of his best friend, who's totally girl-crazy but hasn't even realized who the right girl for him is, but now she's gotten jealous, and...Earth to Harry! Earth to Harry! The dating scene at your school sucks! So stop obsessing on the nearest thing with a warm pulse, before you lose yours! They're trying to kill you, dummy! Ahhhh, there's no doubt about it...

Harry

Such **nightmarish destruction!** Oh God, why is this **happening?**

Because **otherwise**, the **first hour** of this **movie** would be as **talky** and **uneventful** as the **first hundred pages** of the **book!**

What a **nightmare**, to see a **shambling**, **undead creature** on the **loose** in the streets of **London!** And behind **Amy Winehouse**, I see a **Death Eater!**

I am **Alpo Hussein Doubledork**, the avuncular **Headmaster** for the **Halfwits School of Wizardry and Window Repair!** Give me an **11-year-old** to teach, and I'll **return** them at the age of **18!** Frequently, in a **body bag!** In the last **five years**, no fewer than **six** Halfwits professors have **injured, terrorized** or **murdered** our students. It's part of my **"No Child Left Alive"** program! It sounds **exotic**, but many **American kids** have a **7-year-long education**. Unfortunately, they call it **"high school"!**

The **wizard** behind this **attack**, **Lord Druckermort**, was my **most gifted pupil!** He finished **first** in his **class!** Actually, he was **twelfth**, so he **killed** the **eleven kids** ahead of him!

Which brings us to the **three BFF's!** Which stands for **"Beaverface, Fussbudget, and Frownypants"!** **Runt, Herwhiny**, and **Harry!**

Harry Plodder is the hero with the **lightning bolt** on his **head** and the **fog** in his **brain!** I confess that **Harry** has always been my **pet student.** Although when I say **"pet,"** think **Michael Vick!** This semester will be Harry's **darkest.** He must face an **almost impossible challenge** — getting a **girl hot!** It will be interesting to see whether he'll succeed in **losing his virginity**, or get **killed** first. Either way, it'll be **over** in a **flash!**

When **Runt** first arrived, he was a **short, awkward, repulsive, inadequate dweeb!** Five years later, he's not as **short!** Nevertheless, **Runt Queasy** is one of the **all-time great sidekicks!** Just like **Patrick the starfish**, minus the **sex appeal!**

100

WRITER: DESMOND DEVLIN   ARTIST: HERMANN MEJIA

PLODDER IS A HOT-BLOODED PUTZ

Allow me to introduce this year's flawed **plot-device-slash-professor, Horace Rugburn!** He's a master of **potions**, from **Felix Felicis** to **Polyjuice**. And he brews up a mean glass of **crunk juice!** But the **hardest** thing to swallow is **Rugburn's** tale of tutoring **Druckermort** in **dark magic!** For the last **15 years**, since the **Great Wizarding Wars**, he's been in **hiding!** But not because of **guilt**. Because of **bookies!** He **bet** on **Lord Druckermort**, with the **points!**

The repressed **sourpuss** with the **30-year scowl** is **Severely Snapped!** The only thing **oilier** than his **personality** is his **hair!** In fact, his **barber's motto** is "**Drill, baby, drill!**"

Those are the **Malformeds**, a **disgusting, terrible family!** They're like an **albino version** of the **Jonas Brothers!**

Laugh it up while you can, **Fuzzface! I've** been **hand-picked** to **kill** you this semester! **Who better** for this **all-important secret mission** than a **vitamin-deficient hothead** who was **punched out** by a **13-year-old girl?** No doubt about it, **Lord Druckermort** has all the **strategic planning skills** of **Napoleon.** Not **Bonaparte...Dynamite!**

The always diligent **Miss Grungy** has read **every book** in the **Halfwits library, twice!** The only one she **couldn't finish** was the **fourth book** in the **Twilight** series. What a **stinker** THAT was! The bland **tweeners**, the **flat** and **repetitive writing**, the **played-out fantasy world scenario**, the **corny romance...er...forget** I **mentioned** it!

Harry, I have an **overwhelming sense** of **dread** and **hopelessness** about the **future!**

It looks **bad**, but stay **optimistic!**

I **can't! I've read** the **seventh book!** And I've got an **open-mouthed kissing scene** with **Runt!** *Gack!* Couldn't we do a quick **rewrite**, and let the **Death Eaters** zap the **crap** out of me?

I'll **do** it — I'll make the **Unbearable Vow** that **binds** me to your son **Drano!** Let's **spit** on our **hands** and touch **pinkie fingers!** But why would you **sign away** your **only son** to a **remorseless fiend?** Why **volunteer** him as the **Dark Lord's** eternal **puppet slave?**

We've always wanted **Drano** to go into the **family business!**

How does it feel to be as **frozen** and **useless** as **David Blaine?** You can't **move** a **muscle!** Unsurprisingly, your **acting chops** are the **same** as ever! I bet you're **sorry** you **snuck out** of your **safe** little **train compartment** now!

No! Runt's in there watching *Beverly Hills Chihuahua*... again!

Harry, using that special **Potions textbook** is **cheating!** Worse, you were already almost **killed** by a **mysterious book** that appeared from an **unknown benefactor. Remember** finding young **Druckermort's** planted **diary?** And your **battle** in the **Chamber of Secrets?** And the **giant snake** that drove its **fangs** into your **flesh?**

Mmm... **nope!** Sorry, it doesn't **ring a bell!**

Harry, check out this moldy old **memory** of when I first met **Tom Riddler**...

A **weird old coot** in a **bathrobe** wants to **adopt** a **12-year-old boy** and take him away to a **secluded castle?** I don't see **why not!**

I've **never told** anyone, but I can **move things!** I can **hurt people!** I can **talk to snakes!** And I **touch myself** during *Dora the Explorer!*

Waaaaaaay too much **information!** But I'll take him anyway — pack him up!

They're guarding **Druckermort's herplex**. I've never seen a **mindless, dead-eyed army** of **skeletons** like this!

I have! On *America's Next Top Model!* But what you're **drinking** is **hurting** you! I know you have to swallow **every drop** of this **ghastly green potion**, sir. But it's just **too horrible! Stop!**

No, **Harry**, I must **continue**, despite the **agony**! **Mountain Dew** may taste like **goat piss**, but I'm going to need the **electrolytes**!

Say **hello** to my **leetle friend!** Earn this...**earn** it. Neo, I'm not **afraid** anymore. FREEEEEEDOM!!!! The **horror**. The **horror!** I'll **never** let go, Jack, I **promise**. I don't **deserve** this. I was **building** a **house**. I'm **melting! Melting!** Never go in against a **Sicilian** when **death** is on the line, ha ha ha ha ha! *Rosebud!* If you **strike me down**, Darth, I will become **more powerful** than you can possibly **imagine**. The **coin** don't have no **say!**

What the hell are you **doing**?

Ad libbing! This is my big, unforgettable **death scene!** And all the **script** has me say is **"Aagh!"**

Yes! *I* am the **Half-Blood Prince!** Which explains my **pasty, washed-out complexion!** But know **one thing** before I **flee!** I **never** wasn't not **no one** that **neither** you nor **Doubledork** couldn't **un-trust!** There! **That'll** keep the **fanboys guessing!**

I'll **hunt** you down, **Professor!** I'll avenge **Doubledork's murder** if it takes me a **whole other movie** to **do** it!

You're going to need **two** of 'em!

Oh, Harry! **Alpo Doubledork** is **dead!** Who'll **protect** you **now**?

Are you **kidding?** *He's* the guy who made me **fight** a fire-breathing **dragon** for **no good reason!** Every **teacher** *he* hires tries to **kill** me! He brought **Druckermort** into this school in the **first place!** With **Doubledork** out of the way, I've got a **fighting chance** to **stay alive!**

105

Multiple Personality Disorder is defined as "a condition in which two or more distinct personalities alternately prevail in the same person." Which means we think you'll alternately love/hate this funny/boring article by one of our most beloved/hated and smart/hammerheaded creators/hacks. It's...

JOHN CALDWELL'S
The Multifaceted Upside of Having a Multiple Personality Disorder in School

WRITER AND ARTIST: JOHN CALDWELL

The principal is forever on the defensive because he's never certain who's been sent to his office: the absent-minded slacker with a heart of gold, or the psycho Ritalin abuser teetering on the brink

When it comes to the school debate team, you know those people who say you can't have it both ways? Well, you can

Way more hall passes than the average student

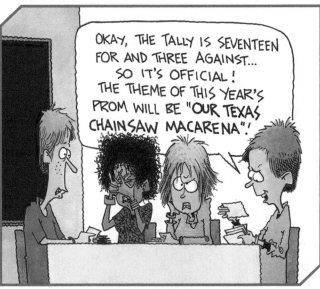

You get to cast the deciding votes on the prom committee

While the other morons in class are buying highly traceable thesis papers on the internet, you have the advantage of calling upon "Hans," your highly prolific rocket scientist persona

At recess, you're technically never the last one chosen for sports

You have a lower risk factor when it comes to passing notes in class

Multiple nicknames

Summer means just one thing! Complete, constant freedom… for about a day or so. Then, if you want to actually do anything, you'll need a job to pay for it! But just because you've got to work, that doesn't mean you have to take the first job that comes along! Before you agree to put on that hairnet and plastic smock, here are some…

THINGS TO CONSIDER BEFORE

What are the hook-up possibilities?

Are there any, um, inmates or whatever, that are under, like, thirty? Or even forty?

How lame are the uniforms?

Cumbersome?!? Your dress is too *cumbersome*? Maybe you should take a minute — off the clock — and think about the REAL pioneer women and how they'd kick your lazy, cumbersome ass!!!

PRAIRIE DOGS

Is there cell phone reception?

Hold on — we're going through the freakin' tunnel again!

Will you be able to get there and back?

Hi, Mrs. Norbert? Um, this is Bradley Kwirk — 'member, from Webelos a few years ago?…Well, I was wondering if you could give me a lift…

BEEFY Bob's

Are the fringe benefits cool or sucky?

…and at the end of the season, you fellas get to keep all the stained tablecloths!!

decent

108

WRITER AND ARTIST: TERESA BURNS PARKHURST

Anyone familiar with Yu-Gi-Oh! knows that over the past few years, the hot cards that fans clamored for were the Egyptian god monsters and the sacred beasts. However, gods and monsters exist in the real world, too — unfortunately, more monsters than gods! Here's...

CELEBRITY Yu-Gi-Oh!

Yu-Gi-O'Reilly

[BLOVIATOR / OFFENSIVE / LEVEL: 10 / MORON]
A fiend with dark powers for confusing the enemy with half-truths and bluster. Its signature attack consists of spinning the facts to suit its position and diving from out of the Right to attack opponents' patriotism. Using this card decreases player's intelligence significantly. Play this card in Attack position facing Left.

Yu-Gi-Oprah

[RICH RICH / LEVEL: 10 / VAIN]
A vain, perpetually dieting enchantress with limitless power that taps into the dark forces of the intellectually helpless by brainwashing them with a sickening touchy-feely style. The most powerful alpha female card in the deck.

Yu-Gi-Osama

[DEMON / EVIL / LEVEL: 10 / ELUSIVE]
An attack from this creature has earth-shaking results. As long as this card remains hidden it is impervious to any spell cards opponents can play. Increase your After-Life Points 1,000 fold after each explosive act of self-inflicted martyrdom and attempted capture. This demon rules over death, and administers it when necessary. Absolutely merciless when facing infidels.

Yu-Gi-O'Donnell

[ANNOYING / FAT LEVEL: 8 / IDIOT]
What this creature lacks in intelligence it makes up for in size, yet continues to make enemies when opening cavernous oral cavity. You can bypass her defense by playing the Trump card.

CARDS

Yu-Gi-O.J.

[FRIGHTENING / GUILTY / LEVEL: 2 / LUNATIC]
Play this card to execute a powerful attack and send former allies to the Graveyard without the slightest trace of guilt. Destroy multiple lives and remove them from play. Use this card without conscience or penalty. Most effective when placed between black and white cards, but if the card doesn't fit, you must quit.

i-Obama

[HOPEFUL / SAVIOR / LEVEL: 10 / DEMOCRAT]
Possibly the strongest card in the deck but if played too early it will lose some of its power. Broad fan base allows for taking control of the battlefield and capturing opponents' red cards.

Yu-Gi-Olsen Twins

[SKINNY SAD / LEVEL: 10 / SCARY]
Mesmerized by this monster's merchandising ability, opponents are spellbound and paralysis ensues. Despite emaciated appearances, the ghastly vampire zombie sisters still control an immense entertainment empire. These siblings once possessed the ability to appear as the same person when their house was full, but these tabloid gossip socialites have recently fallen from grace and their power has been diminished.

Yu-Gi-O'Neal

[BIG, REALLY BIG / LEVEL: 9 / REALLY, REALLY BIG!]
His battle-charge is a force to be reckoned with. Nothing can stop the mad attack of this powerful creature. He destroys all opponents, but if fouled, his return shots will be ineffective and he will be unable to score.

Yu-Gi-Opie & Anthony

[INDECENT / OFFENSIVE / LEVEL: 1 / SHOCKING]
Activate this card to violate decency standards while cloaking yourself behind a first amendment defense. Target males in the 18-49 demographic with sophomoric discourse and deplorable comments that a significant portion of society finds offensive, including thinly veiled or excused racism, homophobia, exploitation of women and ridicule of the disabled to make opponents cringe.

WRITER:
MICHAEL ARNOLD

ARTIST:
TOM RICHMOND

THE ELDERLY

PROS

- The hip, high-tech design means it will never be mistaken for your insulin pump.

- Yes, there's a Bingo App.

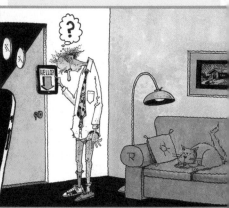

Customizable home page means you can leave yourself a daily reminder to wear pants.

CONS

- Unlike your customized, pimped-out Jazzy Scooter, Medicare won't pay for it.

When reading, the old habit of licking fingers before turning pages can sometimes result in mild electrocution.

- Google is utterly useless when searching for misplaced dentures.

BOTTOM LINE:
Need we repeat, Grandpa?
MEDICARE WON'T PAY FOR IT!

iPud

MAD RATES THE iPAD FOR VARIOUS DEMOGRAPHICS

WRITER AND ARTIST: JOHN CALDWELL

PLUMBERS

PROS

- Who's to know you're stretching your hourly rate by watching movies under the sink?

Easily stored while you're working.

- Access to unlimited and complex industry data means you'll never again screw up the "lefty loosey, righty tighty" rule.

CONS

- It's really depressing that your excellent rubber washer replacement videos just never seem to go viral.

- The built-in high tech calendar is no match for your ol' school "PVC Pipe Dancing Bikini Babes" paper edition.

It doesn't float.

BOTTOM LINE:
It's like flushing a grand down the toilet.

SUPER MODELS

PROS

- Instant web access means no more wondering how many calories there are in a single raisin.

- Frequent crashes, glitches and screen freezes are bound to bring out your sexiest pouts.

Just click on iBooks, select a hefty volume, then balance that bad boy on your head for a little high-tech poise practice.

CONS

- Touch screen technology is a real nail-breaker.

There's no getting around the fact that it's thinner than you'll ever hope to be.

- $500 is a lot to spend on something that — let's face it — you're mostly going to be doing lines of coke off.

BOTTOM LINE:
This thing is already so April 2010.

MOB GUYS

PROS

A giant step in bringing the perp walk into the 21st century.

- We were surprised to learn there's an App available for determining who's wearing a wire.

- Built-in GPS means that you always know where the bodies are buried.

CONS

- You find out the hard way that the oath of Omerta also applies to Tweets.

Once all the guys have one, it becomes necessary to keep a made cyber geek around for tech support.

- They don't make a shoulder holster for the damn thing.

BOTTOM LINE:
Not for nothin', but this is a @#$*in' offer we could easily refuse.

FUNERAL DIRECTORS

PROS

- FAQs like, "Why is this a closed casket service?" can now be answered on the spot and in high definition.

- The chance to tag on an additional fee for iPad-friendly version of online obit? Ka-ching!

Easy access to old Facebook photos is a big help in making the deceased look natural.

CONS

- The complexion of wakes and services change drastically once word gets out that your funeral parlor is a WiFi hotspot.

It turns out that an iPad photo gallery of the embalming process is not the selling point you thought it would be.

- Tech support glitches could easily result in some guy named Mohammed showing up to speak at the Ginzberg service.

BOTTOM LINE:
Our condolences to anyone who buys this piece of crapola.

HITCHHIKERS

PROS

Spell-check especially helpful for destinations like Minneaplias and Cinsinatti.

- Photo application provides room for a handy thumbnail gallery of thumbs.

- Built-in GPS lets you know if the trucker who picked you up might be a serial killer headed to a desolate location.

CONS

- So, since this thing isn't a cell phone, what are you going to do if the trucker who picked you up is indeed a serial killer headed for a desolate location?

- Eats up considerably more of your traveling budget than a Sharpie and some empty pizza box found in a dumpster.

Be aware that a shiny reflective screen coupled with just the right angle of the sun, can turn a potential ride into a 70-mile-an-hour, two-ton sayonara.

BOTTOM LINE:
A hitchhiker's thumb down!

PIRATES

PROS

- Availability of Google Maps eliminates the need for bulky treasure maps.

There's a sweet doubloon conversion App.

- Brings a whopping five dollars (U.S.) at the local open bazaar. (Somali pirates only.)

CONS

- Hook leaves unsightly scratches on the screen.

The necessity of WiFi accessibility means goodbye pints of rum and hello Starbucks macchiatos.

- Unwieldy touch screen keyboard means cutting way down on the number of AAAAARRRRGHs in your emails.

BOTTOM LINE:
The iPad walks the plank.

Introduced in 2004, *World of Warcraft* has become the most successful MMORPG ever. Set in a world of hot flowing lava, ancient evils, mythical creatures and endless bloody conflicts, to the casual observer WoW may seem like nothing more than a cheesy attempt to exploit the empty lives of downtrodden individuals by catering to their blood-lust fantasies at a fee of $15 per month. But it's more – much, much more. And if you give us enough time, we'll figure out what that "more" is and get back to you. In the meantime, if you've ever wondered what 12 million-plus people are doing every night on their computers *besides* looking at porn, here's…

MAD's HANDY QUICK PRIMER TO WORLD OF WARCRAFT™

WoW: THE BACKSTORY!

Ten thousand years before the First War between the orcs and the humans, the world of Azeroth was sundered, and a storm raged where the Well of Eternity once stood. The various races each pursued their own destinies in this perilous new realm. A great battle erupted to determine which sect would control the supply of unobtainium, and many Na'vi perished. Plankton failed in his quest to claim the recipe for the Krusty Krab burger. Hamlet avenged the murder of his father, but would not live to see the new era. Kelly Monaco claimed the crown with her natural grace, but was soon unseated by the ruthless Drew Lachey. Traversing distant lands, Edward and Bella were captured by the Volturi. Woody and Buzz nearly perished in the Great Furnace, and were only rescued through an uneasy alliance with the squeaky green aliens.

FUN FACT!

"MMORPG" STANDS FOR MASSIVE MULTI-PLAYER ONLINE ROLE PLAYING GAME. COINCIDENTALLY, IT'S ALSO THE SOUND A PLAYER MAKES WHILE EXTRACTING THEIR ASS FROM THEIR CHAIR, AFTER PLAYING FOR SEVEN HOURS STRAIGHT.

WRITER: DESMOND DEVLIN   ARTIST: HERMANN MEJIA

CREATING YOUR CHARACTER!

With 10 types of Races, 10 different Classes, and 11 Primary Professions, there are over a thousand possibilities for your own unique character! Just try not to think about the existing 12 million subscribers out there, meaning that no matter how long you plan or what you decide, there are already more than 12,000 duplicates of your "unique" character in the game. All with more experience than you.

FUN FACT!

THE GAME ALLOWS YOU TO BUILD YOUR CHARACTER'S STRENGTH AND AGILITY AS YOUR REAL-LIFE MUSCLE TONE TURNS TO NERF.

GAME PLAY!

The WoW experience is designed to be a true-to-life, intricate communal model with all the subtle nuances of a genuine working civilization, providing limitless avenues for your character to interact with the social strata, based entirely on your character's goals and choices. So think carefully: do you prefer zapping people, or stabbing them?

FUN FACT!

WoW ALLOWS YOU TO ENTER INTO RELATIONSHIPS WITH LITTLE ANIMATED DWARVES WHO WILL COME TO MEAN MORE TO YOU THAN YOUR OWN FAMILY.

FOLLOWING THE ACTION!

Everything you need to know is right on your screen! At any given time, you'll see text describing your character's position and actions, information about all stationary and mobile objects in the immediate vicinity, an omen threat meter, area maps with possible flight paths, a constantly-updated status bar, damage reports and attack results, quest logs, icons for each of the items in your inventory and also for unclaimed quest items, your totals of gold and mana, an auctioneer add-on which tracks prices for items you wish to sell or purchase, text messages from other characters, screen notations listing characters' arrivals and departures, as well as other advanced options.

Once you get the hang of game play, keeping an eye on this all-important information will become second nature!

You have joined the Pillowfight Guild

JOINING A GUILD!

There's nothing like the personal satisfaction of being a valued part of a unified team. That way, you can hang back as your teammates rush into one of those impossible dungeon killing fields, and let those other pseudonymous meatsacks absorb 95% of the damage!

But every guild is different, so don't be afraid to try several of them out. You may not be satisfied with your first guild, or your second, or your tenth, but you can move on. It will take time, perhaps years, but just keep looking until you find the perfect match for you. Did we mention the $15 monthly fee?

FUN FACT!
WoW TAKES THE TWIN ACTIVITIES OF TYPING AND WANDERING AROUND, AND COMBINES THEM INTO SOMETHING EVEN MORE EXCITING!

SHARING YOUR KNOWLEDGE

After playing for two days, it's time to proclaim yourself an expert by making your own boastful advice video and posting it on YouTube! Here's some tips to make your video the best ever!

✦ Label your video "WORLD RECORD!!!!" to make it stand out from the other 400,000 videos labelled "World Record."

✦ Always sound authoritative, even when you're offering staggeringly useless advice.

✦ Be sure to add a pounding hard rock song blasting in the background for the duration of your video. (To decide on the music, take a look at several hundred of the other videos, and then choose one of the five songs they all use.)

✦ Remember, if your video gets watched enough, you will have achieved the one thing every *World of Warcraft* player dreams of doing: bringing in new players even more inept and clueless than yourself, so you can kill them.

Okay, now I'm here... you need to open this door...okay... mm-hmm...and as you can see, there it is.

HOW "WORLD OF WARCRAFT" IS JUST LIKE BEING A BLOOD OR A CRIP!

✦ EVERYBODY GETS A NICKNAME.

✦ PLAYERS SPEND ALL THEIR TIME EITHER HANGING AROUND OR FIGHTING.

✦ SLASHINGS ARE CONDONED.

✦ BODY ARMOR OFFERS ONLY PARTIAL PROTECTION.

✦ YOU NEED TO JOIN A GANG TO STAY ALIVE.

✦ A PLAYER'S STATUS IS DETERMINED BY HOW MUCH BLING THEY'VE GOT.

✦ MEMBERS ARE INCARCERATED INSIDE THEIR ROOMS/CELLS, DOING MIND-NUMBINGLY REPETITIVE TASKS.

BONUS FEATURE!
A LOOK AT THE NEWEST EDITION...

WORLD of WARCRAFT CATACLYSM

Everyone's talking about the newest, hottest, most sizzling destination in the world of video games. Unfortunately, it's *StarCraft II: Wings of Liberty*. Meanwhile, this is just another place with lava.

With the release of *World of Warcraft: Cataclysm*, the vistas of this amazing world open up at least another 1% or 2%. An update of this magnitude hasn't been seen since they stuck eyelashes and a hair ribbon on Pac-Man and called it a brand new game.

FEATURES OF WORLD OF WARCRAFT: CATACLYSM!

✦ Blizzard Entertainment game developers spent 5 years and $3 million getting Kalimdor to look like a rock.

✦ The Sunken City of Vash'jir has a surprisingly good school system.

✦ Gamers can now play as goblins or werewolves — but WoW's limited graphics technology makes most players end up looking like Snooki or Russell Brand, respectively.

✦ New in-game ballot initiative gives players a chance to sign a petition to change the name of Shadowfang Keep to "Happydale Glen."

HOT NEW GEAR!

There are only so many eldritch scrolls and enchanted elixirs you can buy before you feel like just another Glenn Beck viewer who's realized that hoarding gold is ultimately meaningless. Luckily, there are snazzy NEW items in the game to buy, which are limited only by how many of them there are!

✦ A special three-handed axe. You'll never be able to use it!

✦ A LeBron James Miami Heat jersey

✦ Mystically unspoilable mayonnaise

✦ Those crazy birthday candles that keep re-igniting

✦ Extra apostrophes to make ordinary words seem more ex'otic

✦ The chattering teeth – always funny!

Sure, just last year, we ran an article entitled "Don't You Hate When Your Parents..." – but with parents doing so many stupid, annoying and infuriating things, there's no way *one* article could cover it all! Besides, summer is all about terrible sequels (We're looking at you, *Daddy Day Care!*) which is why we're forcing you to read...

DON'T YOU HATE WHEN YOUR PARENTS...
THE SEQUEL!

...make you feel like dirt for not wanting to visit your grandparents, despite secretly loathing the visits ten times worse than you?

...complain about "how easy you have it," as if *they* grew up in a Chinese sweatshop and not a suburban house with zone air-conditioning, bean-bag chairs and a puke-green rumpus room?

...threaten you with twenty kinds of death if they ever catch you "using drugs," despite not being able to survive a single day without caffeine, alcohol or ibuprofen?

...assure you that "it's what's inside that counts" — yet whine endlessly about the way you dress?

WRITER: JACOB LAMBERT   ARTIST: DAVE CROSLAND

...whine about the stuff that you find funny — while routinely plastering the fridge with *Ziggy*, *Cathy* and *Beetle Bailey* cartoons?

...won't let you have a dog because "you're not responsible enough" — a qualification that somehow didn't keep them from having you?

...buy you gifts that prove how little they actually know you — then try to make you feel guilty for your "ungratefulness"?

...complain that you don't read enough — then, when you do, complain that you aren't reading the "right" things?

Everyone thinks **Justin Bieber** is SOOOOO great.

But how great is he REALLY?

Let's settle this once and for all
with a little feature we like to call:

BIEBER

BIEBER VS. **BEAKER**

Winner:
BEAKER!

Incomprehensible, high-pitched muppet
has a much less annoying voice.

BIEBER VS. **BABAR**

Winner:
BABAR!

"King of the Elephants" outranks
"Prince of the Bowl Cuts."

BIEBER VS. **BUBLÉ**

Winner:
IT'S A TIE!

Both produce equally-
crappy music.

BIEBER VS. **BEEMER**

Winner:
BEEMER!

Sophisticated German automobile
requires less engineering and production
than the average Bieber single.

BIEBER VS. **BOO BERRY**

Winner:
BOO BERRY!

Boo Berry exhibits far more
personality, despite being dead.

BIEBER VS. **BOMBSHELL**

Winner:
IT'S A TIE!

Both of their photos are used
as currency in prison.

BIEBER VS. **BEBOP**

Winner:
IT'S A TIE!

Bebop is a mutated half-human/
half-warthog. Bieber is Canadian.

BIEBER VS. **BUDDHA**

Winner:
BUDDHA!

Buddha's followers aren't going
to stop giving a s#*% about him
as soon as they turn 17.

BIEBER VS. **BUBBA**

Winner:
BUBBA!

Bieber's position on curbing
nuclear proliferation in Iran and other
Middle East countries is naïve at best.

VERSUS...

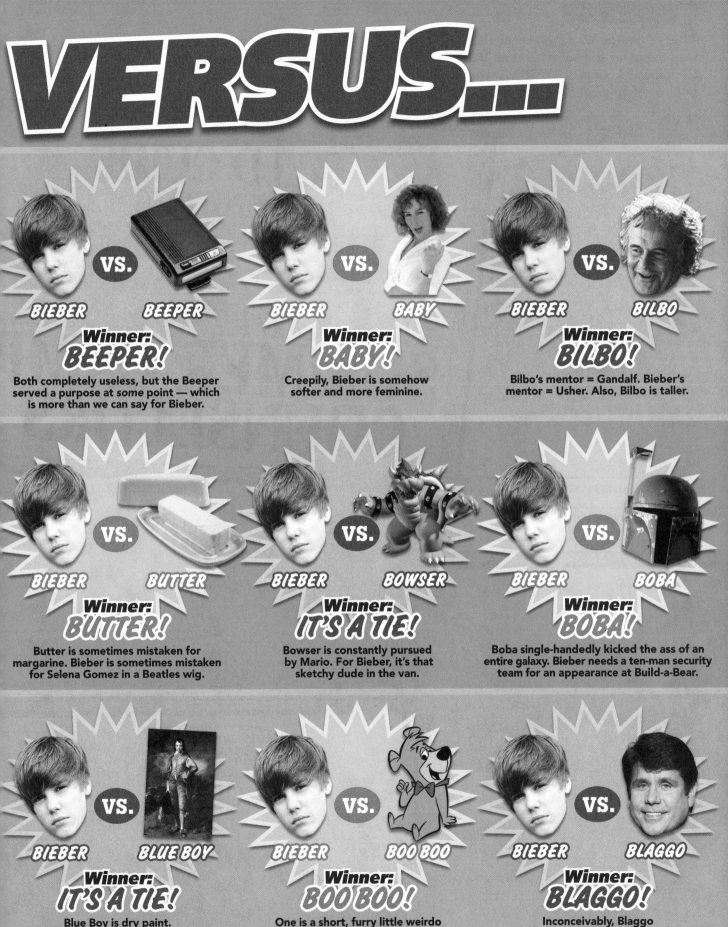

BIEBER VS. **BEEPER**

Winner:
BEEPER!
Both completely useless, but the Beeper served a purpose at *some* point — which is more than we can say for Bieber.

BIEBER VS. **BABY**

Winner:
BABY!
Creepily, Bieber is somehow softer and more feminine.

BIEBER VS. **BILBO**

Winner:
BILBO!
Bilbo's mentor = Gandalf. Bieber's mentor = Usher. Also, Bilbo is taller.

BIEBER VS. **BUTTER**

Winner:
BUTTER!
Butter is sometimes mistaken for margarine. Bieber is sometimes mistaken for Selena Gomez in a Beatles wig.

BIEBER VS. **BOWSER**

Winner:
IT'S A TIE!
Bowser is constantly pursued by Mario. For Bieber, it's that sketchy dude in the van.

BIEBER VS. **BOBA**

Winner:
BOBA!
Boba single-handedly kicked the ass of an entire galaxy. Bieber needs a ten-man security team for an appearance at Build-a-Bear.

BIEBER VS. **BLUE BOY**

Winner:
IT'S A TIE!
Blue Boy is dry paint. Watching a Bieber performance is as exciting as watching paint dry.

BIEBER VS. **BOO BOO**

Winner:
BOO BOO!
One is a short, furry little weirdo that probably poops in the woods. The other is a delightful animated bear.

BIEBER VS. **BLAGGO**

Winner:
BLAGGO!
Inconceivably, Blaggo has better hair!

After spending all school year listening to stupid, boring and clueless teachers, is there any better way to spend the summer than listening to obnoxious, boring and clueless camp counselors? Of course! Almost ANYTHING would be better! But going to camp is your parents' decision, not yours, buddy! So at least you can tell the jerks apart, thanks to...

JOHN CALDWELL'S
FIELD GUIDE
TO SPOTTING
AMERICA'S MOST INCOMPETENT SUMMER CAMP COUNSELORS

LONNIE SHEAF
Camp Hornswagle, Indiana
Insists on diving board "dry runs" for the weaker swimmers.

MMMF....SORRY ABOUT THAT.

LEON BURLINGAME
Camp Nap-N-Noodle, Montana
Suffers from a bad case of pottery wheel motion sickness.

GAHAAAAGH...

FWIRF GURG BLIRT GURG

WOW! CHECK IT OUT, GUYS! AN ANCIENT CHEROKEE JUICE BOX!

BONGO AKIMBO

CHESTER CURDLER
Camp Fester, Kansas
His knowledge of Native American artifacts is sketchy, to say the least.

OKSANA FANTAUZZI
Camp Wak-A-Vole, Connecticut
Her S'mores have been linked to an outbreak of what doctors are calling "S'malmonella."

ARNOLD "LAMBCHOP" HACKENBERRY
Camp Wasabi, Texas
Before making crafts from popsicle sticks, campers must first wait for him to eat all the popsicles.

LÜF HARKINSCHŸEN
Camp Trailmicks, Oregon
His scary campfire stories always center around mutual funds gone bad.

HARRIET WURTZEL
Camp Tickhaven, Massachusetts
Organizes relay races with scissors.

CARLA P. DECATUR
Camp Skankwater, South Carolina
The only so-called "Indian Lore" she ever passes on is how to buy cartons of Winstons at deep discounts.

BURNE FILLMORE
Camp Pluck-A-Chuck, New Hampshire
Holds only one nature session, which focuses solely on what to do when it calls.

The seventh movie in the Harry Plodder saga, the seventh MAD spoof of the boy wizard. At this point, all you need to know is: It's...

Harry

The **boy** is **all alone** and **vulnerable**. But we can't blast **Plodder** to **pieces** until he **physically** leaves his **house**, because it's **protected** by the potent **Stretchio Convenius charm!** That **spell** can only be created by combining **powerful magic**, a **dying mother's love**, and an **author** who didn't want her **$8 billion franchise** to come to a **screeching halt** on **Book Seven, Page Two!**

My Lord Druckermort, I bring you **news!** They will be moving **Harry Plodder** this **Wednesday** night. We must travel there to **attack!**

You mean to **say...?**

Yes — we shall have to TiVo *Cougar Town!*

In the **battle** between the **purebloods** and the **mudbloods**, we **Malformeds** are *no-bloods!* Our **entire family** only has one **red corpuscle** between us. *I* get to use it on **Tuesdays** and **Fridays!** If **Drano** had been born a **girl**, we would have named her **Anemia!** I'm so **angry** and so **white**, I'm the **odds-on** favorite to capture the **Tea Party's presidential nomination!**

Lord Druckermort is the most **diabolical wizard** in **history**, but he's an even *more* **unbearable house guest!** He **abuses** and **insults** us. He opens **new cereal** when there are already **open boxes** that aren't **finished**. And he's been ordering **pay-per-view** programming, on *our* cable bill! I mean, **who** pays to watch *MacGruber* **five days in a row?**

Being the **youngest Death Eater** is **tough!** Sometimes I wish I were a **regular kid** with a normal **summer vacation**. I've never even been to **Disney World!** Instead, I'm stuck with **ugly strangers** and **oversized animals**, hanging around some **old castles** and **sweating** like a **pig**. On second thought, this is *exactly* like going to **Disney World!**

Check it out! With these **3-D glasses**, you can **almost see** the boss' **nose!**

Who cares! **Druckermort** gives me the **creeps**. Besides the **skinless nostrils**, he's got those **slits** for **eyes** with **no eyebrows**, that waxy **see-through flesh**, those veiny **temples**, that **clenched jaw** with **missing lips**...

Eh, whatever. It's *still* **better** than the work **Bruce Jenner** had done!

WRITER: DESMOND DEVLIN   ARTIST: TOM RICHMOND

Plodder
AND IT'S DREADFUL WHAT FOLLOWS
To fool Druckermort, six of you have become exact duplicates of Harry Plodder. Suddenly the room just got 700% nerdier!
At long last, Harry Plodder in a bra! Hmm. Somehow, this isn't as sexy as the online fanfic made it seem!
WANTED: ACTING JOBS (NO SCARS)
What are you doing, Herwhiny?
Just satisfying my curiosity about something... yup! Just what I thought! You're not even close to being the greatest wizard of them all!

SEZ EDUCATION DEPT.

Your teachers talk, talk, talk. All day long, they drone on about denominators and zygotes and hidden meanings in *A Separate Peace*. It's enough to make you feel good that you never listen to a word they say! But, in the unlikely event that you actually pay attention for a second or two, well, then you should be able to understand them! That's why you absolutely need…

MAD's TEACHER TRANSLATION GUIDE

When a teacher says…
"You should all use *her* as an example."

HE *REALLY* MEANS…

Why can't you *all* be brown-nosing suck-ups?

When a teacher says…
"Students today just don't concentrate."

SHE *REALLY* MEANS…

I need to blame my crushing dullness on *something!*

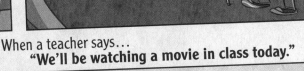

When a teacher says…
"Hmm… I disagree with you, but we don't really have the time to get into it."

SHE *REALLY* MEANS…

CRAP! You're smarter than me!

When a teacher says…
"We'll be watching a movie in class today."

HE *REALLY* MEANS…

I'm *far* too hung over to actually teach!

132

WRITER: JACOB LAMBERT   ARTIST: JOSE GARIBALDI

In a desperate effort to "maintain quality control" (Note: you can't "maintain" something that doesn't exist!), fast food dumps are now encouraging

A FAST FOOD CUSTOMER

WELCOME!

VALU-MEALS

BREAKFAST SPECIALS

HEALTHY ALTERNA-CHOICES

EMPLOYEE OF THE MONTH MAY 2003

http://www.

Thank you for filling out our online customer satisfaction survey.

Please enter comments in the yellow boxes provided.

Para continuar en español, empuje aqui.

When did you visit our restaurant?
○ Today ○ Yesterday ● Other

Months ago. I just keep logging on here every few days trying to win that $1,000 the receipt promises.

Did one of our employees greet you?
○ Yes ● No

While an employee didn't greet me, a guy panhandling for spare change between the drive-thru lane and just outside the door did.

Was your order taken promptly?
● Yes ○ No

By "yes" I mean that I was abruptly asked what I wanted to order the very second I opened the door, while I was standing 20 feet from the counter and hadn't even looked at the menu board.

Did you order breakfast from our breakfast menu?
○ Yes ● No

I tried to, because the breakfast menu was still on display, but your employee said they stopped serving breakfast twelve seconds before I got there.

Did our server tell you about our exciting new menu items?
● Yes ○ No

If you mean "Was the mandatory practice of forcing our employees to lifelessly recite some come-on scrawled on an index card taped to the register to somehow convince you to try whatever new, overpriced and unhealthy combination of meat, cheese and jalapeño peppers we're pushing this month enforced?" then I suppose that'd be "Yes."

Are you aware of our Healthy Alternachoices™ menu items?
○ Yes ● No

You must be kidding! If I was interested in eating "healthy," do you really think I'd be coming in here?

WRITER: SCOTT MAIKO   ARTIST: PETER BAGGE

their undernourished patrons to go online and give them feedback about how their "dining" experience was. Consider it done! Here's…

SATISFACTION SURVEY (THAT TELLS IT LIKE IT IS)

McBurgy's

urgys.fastfoodsurvey.com 🔍▾ Search

Did you enjoy the speed and ease of ordering a Valu-Meal by number from our menu board?
○ Yes ● No

"Speed and ease" aren't the phrases that come to mind when your employees routinely confuse a #3 with a #7 and you're half a mile away before you realize that instead of the chicken wrap you wanted, you're stuck with a greasy fish sandwich containing the allergic-reaction-inducing tartar sauce that sends you to the emergency room.

Were our employees attentive in keeping the dining room area neat and clean?
○ Yes ● No

Not so much "attentive" as "obsessive-compulsive," and not so much "the entire dining room area" as "the floor directly beneath my table" which your employee passive-aggressively attempted to vacuum while I tried to eat in peace, as though this was the only time in her entire eight-hour shift that she would have a chance to clean this specific 2-foot by 2-foot area.

Were there salt and pepper shakers on your table?
○ Yes ● No

There were pairs of pepper shakers on all the tables on one side of the restaurant, and pairs of salt shakers on all the tables on the other side, which can probably be attributed to an unattended and bored six-year-old looking for something to do while Mommy finishes her Grilled Baby Cranberry Caesar Ranchero Salad, or an employee who's unfamiliar with the distribution of basic seasonings.

If you requested extra condiments, did you receive…
● …enough ○ …not enough

Let's put it this way: Thanks to the wasteful amount of ketchup your employees evidently believe I need to enhance a medium order of fries, I've finally realized my dream of opening my own restaurant supply business with the surplus.

Was the napkin dispenser on your table stocked with a supply of paper napkins?
● Yes ○ No

"Stocked"? Try "Crammed so tightly with three times the capacity of napkins it was designed to hold that I was physically unable to pull out one as well as afraid that in my attempt to do so, the dispenser would go off like a roadside bomb and take out four booths."

Are you aware that our menu's nutritional information is printed on the back of our tray liners?
● Yes ○ No

I figured it out once the grease from the fries rendered the paper translucent.

Was the restaurant you visited one of our 24-hour locations?
● Yes ○ No

Judging by the prevalence of parasite-infested homeless people pontificating about the government, including one who insisted on showing me a bad magic trick involving a broken cigarette and then harassed me until I bought him a vanilla shake, yes, it was likely a 24-hour location.

Finally, thinking back about your recent visit, was there any particular employee who stood out?
● Yes ○ No

You mean the kid yelling at his girlfriend on his cell phone? Yeah, when I was leaving, he stood out by the side entrance chain-smoking non-filtered Camels while lines were ten deep and one register was open. Unfortunately, now that I've mentioned it, you're going to have to update that "Employee of the Month" plaque whose last addition was in May, 2003.

On a scale from 1 to 5, with 1 being "poor" and 5 being "excellent" how would you rate the cleanliness of…

Our self-service soft drink station?
● 1 ○ 2 ○ 3 ○ 4 ○ 5

There was a camera crew from *National Geographic* videotaping some sort of new life form spotted swimming under that metal grate.

The carpet and/or floor area?
● 1 ○ 2 ○ 3 ○ 4 ○ 5

I had a close-up look when I slipped on one of those loose plastic balls kicked in from the play area and fell on my ass and landed on a discarded mayonnaise-covered lettuce leaf and a puddle of orange soda.

The trash receptacles outside the restaurant?
● 1 ○ 2 ○ 3 ○ 4 ○ 5

I couldn't get close enough to rate them; the raccoons were particularly aggressive.

Maybe it's because of a bad upbringing, a history of drug abuse or traces of zebra dung in the water supply. Whatever the cause, it's not pretty to watch and has the potential to make entire species turn against each other. Here's what happens...

When Mo

OOOH....AMERICAN EXPRESS PLATINUM!

FLIK FLIK FLIK

APRIL 12... THE BIG SILVERBACK FINALLY ACCEPTS ME AS ONE OF HIS OWN...

Uses the charming custom of grooming others as a diversionary tactic for his pickpocketing habit.

He shocks the bejabbers out of the Darwinian Research Team by suddenly walking "erect," if you know what we're saying.

Practices inappropriate use of the prehensile tail.

Incidences of banana peel-related "accidents" become much more commonplace.

BOBO

HUNGRY =
THIRSTY =
POTTY =
PARTY =

After six months of study, the only sign language he retains is that which he learned from Vito the maintenance guy.

FINZER LABS INC.

Writes off more than $1,500 a year in lab monkey tobacco expenses when, in fact, he's been bumming his smokes since 2003.

WRITER AND ARTIST: PETER KUPER

KUPER

The road to the White House is paved with wild accusations and vicious name-calling. The halls of high school also house their share of rumors and taunts, but for some reason, class elections are relatively civil (except, of course, for a occasional pantsing). With all eyes on election coverage this year, the dirty and despicable tactics used in the presidentia race are bound to inspire the political hopefuls running for student government.
Here's what to expect…

WHEN HIGH SCHOOL ELECTIONS ARE RUN LIKE PRESIDENTIAL ELECTIONS

A candidate preferring Sierra Mist to Mountain Dew will be labeled "an elitist."

The level of a candidate's school spirit will be continually called into question.

A candidate will be severely criticized by his opponent for claiming to support the football team but failing to visit injured players after a big game.

A candidate will question her opponent's ability to handle a 3 P.M. phone call

WRITER: NATHANIEL STEIN   ARTIST: JOSE GARIBALDI

It's **not** your **fangs** that frighten me — it's those **freakishly large eyebrows!**

Look, I love my **new hat** — and you look **great** in the jersey. I just can't **believe** you **killed** Yogi Berra!

Man, **every** time I **drink deer blood** it **always** gives me the **runs!**

Yeah, yeah this would **also** be a **great spot** for a **treehouse**...Now can you **please** just take me **home?**

Wow — we have **so much** in common. We **both** love "Rear Defrost"!

JOHN CALDWELL'S
THE RICH REWARDS
CONVENIEN

The current economy has many people making unanticipated and unwanted career changes. If you're a former bank officer, assembly line manager, airline pilot or publishing executive in need of a new job, you may want to consider…

That special "new name tag" smell.

The keen awareness that the lucky break to a promotion is just one I.N.S. raid away.

That "I can't believe they pay me to do this" feeling you get when spending countless hours poking through mug shots trying to I.D. the alleged perp.

In any social situation, when the topic of beef jerky comes up, you're automatically the go-to guy.

The window of romantic possibility that comes with checking a customer's I.D.

Dealing in a diversity of product prices puts you so much higher on the retail food chain than dollar store clerks.

The satisfaction and sense of responsibility inherent in the knowledge that a powerful corporate entity has entrusted you with the keys to the ice machine.

WRITER AND ARTIST: JOHN CALDWELL

The opportunity to actually be paid hourly wages while pursuing your dream of amassing the world's biggest bag of scratch-off lottery shavings.

12 Reasons We Hate Cell Phones

WRITER: BARRY LIEBMANN   ARTIST: PETER BAGGE

Cell phones are everywhere. But, unfortunately, so are idiots. So it's only logical that idiots have cell phones. And when that happens, even something as wonderful, convenient and fun as a cell phone becomes annoying. Don't believe us? Oh, pappy, you certainly will once you check out these...

Hello? *COUGH COUGH* Can I *HACK WHEEZE* talk to *COUGH*...

Having to leave a noisy, crowded restaurant to get a clear signal, only to find yourself lost in a fog of chain smokers.

BASH!

Okay, so a priest, a rabbi and a clam-digger all go into a bar...

So I says to the guy, if you don't have any more room to add extra speakers in my SUV, just take out the airbags!

There's mounting evidence that cell phones cause brain damage — which can be proven just by listening to the conversation of an average cell phone user.

Hey, look — *Avatar!*

Why the obsession with "multi-platform" distribution? Has anyone ever watched an IMAX blockbuster and thought, "Man, I'd love to see this on an iPhone screen the size of a baseball card!"

MOM!!!

I want you to call me the minute you arrive at the party. And call me again when you're heading home. And check in every hour. Actually, just leave me on speakerphone all night.

CLICK CLICK CLICK CLICK *SHLOOP?*

Though cell phones give airline passengers a chance to talk to loved ones during an accident, they also give idiotic air-traffic controllers a chance to talk while on the job — and CAUSE those accidents!

What the hell do you want?!?!

Morons who answer their phone at an inconvenient time, then angrily blame you for calling them.

What stupid A-hole's phone is...Oops!

Cursing out some inconsiderate d-bag whose phone is ringing in the middle of a play/lecture/wedding/funeral... only to realize that the douche is you!

Thinking that a cell phone will give you more freedom — and finding out the exact opposite is true.

Crap-tards who text during the movies. Great! Now we've got everything we need — popcorn, soda, AND a blinding migraine from that light in the corner of our eye for two straight hours!

Hey, FARRRRT sorry I didn't call you back sooner BRRRAP this is the first time SPLASH I've sat down all day. FLUSH!

Finding out that some people make calls even when they're on the toilet.

Paparazzi wannabes who use camera phone technology to immediately document your every embarrassing mistake.

It's terrible — the doctor says my mom's going to need chemo... or maybe it's radiation. I'm not really sure what the difference is, but...

Let's check on my phone!

Annoying Smart Phone users who can't carry on a single conversation without fact-checking something.

Tweet Deta

Sarah Palin

OBAMA DEATH PANELS FOR YOUR DOGS AND KIDS!

Politicians who Tweet. Great, a NEW way for them to lie to us!

The Believability

Harry Potter may be set in a magical world of wizards, flying cars and talking elves, but even so, there's a limit to what readers will swallow! The fact is, some of what ol' J.K. writes is just TOO outlandish (and we're not just talking about that ginger-haired doofus Ron scoring a stone cold fox like Hermione)! Take a look for yourself at...

We can believe that the favorite foods of Hogwarts students magically appear on their plates...

We can believe that Dumbledore hired a werewolf, a half-giant, and even an ex-practitioner of the Dark Arts to teach at his school...

But we CAN'T believe that his liberal hiring policy apparently doesn't extend to ethnic minorities!

But we CAN'T believe that they haven't become broomstick-breaking, lard-ass blobs as a result!

We can believe there's a sport with a flying ball, named Quidditch...

We can believe that Azkaban prison is run by creatures that can suck every good feeling and every happy memory out of you...

But we CAN'T believe that they're running a prison, and not a public school!

But we CAN'T believe there isn't even one Quidditch coach pushing steroids to get his team into the championships!

WRITER: BARRY LIEBMANN　　　**ARTIST: PAUL COKER**

Unbelievability of Harry Potter

We can believe there's a swelling solution that makes objects grow...

But we CAN'T believe that it isn't being sold on the internet to enlarge...well, you know...

We can believe in a flying car that runs on magical powers...

But we CAN'T believe that the big oil cartels haven't had it destroyed, like they did with every other car that runs on an alternative fuel source!

We can believe there's a masochistic elf, Dobby, who runs head-first into walls, beats himself with a desk lamp and irons his own fingers...

But we CAN'T believe that he hasn't been signed up already by the producers of *Jackass!*

We can believe in broomstick-riding wizards, phoenixes, centaurs, unicorns and other weird creatures...

But we CAN'T believe that cramming these musty old mythical creatures into a story could ever be considered original or creative!

The Young Man's Guide to SUCCESSFUL MALL ROMANCE

Yeah, we see you and your friends, slouched around a bench in the food court, wiping boogers on each others' sleeves and wondering why those girls over there won't talk to you. You're in a tough spot (being a MAD reader makes it twice as bad, trust us), but, hey, if Larry the Cable Guy can avoid unemployment and the Red Sox can win the series, maybe even you can pick someone up at the mall! And if this almost statistically impossible scenario actually somehow does happen, you'll probably need to consult...

Play it safe and tell the **truth** about your age — unless you want her to wonder why a 20-year-old needs to be picked up by his mommy at 6:00 sharp.

Yeah, er... my mom's picking me up. I, uh, left my car back at college. Yeah, that's it... college!

Unless you want her to know what an immature dweeb you are right off the bat, stay away from Spencer Gifts.

This stuff would go great with the inflatable weenie and big-boob beanbag I have at home!

If you need to rip one, for God's sake hold it in — don't just wait 'til you're near Nathan's and blame it on the deep-fried hot dog nuggets.

Yowsa... those wieners really smell like farts, huh?

She might actually think you're intelligent if you take her into Barnes & Noble — but not if you sprint out two minutes later with a *Penthouse* jammed in your pants.

WRITER: JACOB LAMBERT
ARTIST: RICH POWELL

153

SERGIO ARAGONES PRESENTS A MAD

WRITER AND ARTIST: SERGIO ARAGONES   COLORIST: TOM LUTH

157

THE UPSIDES TO A NATIONWIDE BEDBUG INFESTATION

Face it, these are desperate times. There's just nothing good to be said about crushing economic hardships, unending terror threats or that new animated MAD show on Cartoon Network. But don't despair. Because there is one burgeoning calamity growing by leaps and box springs that just ain't as bad as it appears. In fact, it has its good points. And we're sure you'll be nodding your red welt-covered head in agreement, once you've read...

YEAH... YOU SHOULD SEE IT! IT'S A '99 BEAUTYREST QUEEN SIZE AND STILL IN THE SHRINK WRAP.

Chez ERNIE

Owning a relatively clean mattress will have the powerful allure once reserved for those who possess expensive cars and penthouse apartments.

BLOT!

In the looks department, bedbugs have it all over ticks.

WRITER AND ARTIST: JOHN CALDWELL

HERE YOU GO, MORTGAGE MONKEY!

WE LEFT A LITTLE SCRATCH IN THE MATTRESS FOR YOU!!

HAAAA!!!

FOR SALE
FORECLOSED

It takes a little bit of the sting (and a lot of the itch) out of a foreclosure.

159

There's a Fox TV show that's getting heavy buzz. It's a concept that's completely original: It's about "Freaks and Geeks" in a "High School Musical" who want "Fame." So "Bring It On!" Okay, maybe it's not so original. In fact, if you like this show, you're clearly...

glee-

r may sound like it's fun and easy,
n't fool yourself — it's a pressure
r! On a daily basis you have to be
funny and thought-provoking!
t's face it, if you're a MAD reader,
NONE of those things! Thankfully,
s one more thing that
not: honest! At least
eans that you can just...

steal these tweets!

I can't find my "Where's Waldo" book. Looks like he's won before we even started...

On Facebook I mark "Like" for as much stuff as possible — it'll make a great cribsheet if I ever have to battle back from amnesia.

Whenever someone says, "You can't get blood from a stone," don't reply. Just smash them in the face with a stone.

I'm making a scrapbook of all my favorite times spent scrapbooking.

Went to a restaurant that had a chocolate fountain. Fortunately, I had Hanukkah coins on me, so I was able to make a wish.

I finally organized my computer's cluttered desktop. Now I have everything in one tidy folder — labeled "Desktop."

What's the best way to tell the world that I'm allergic to the metal they use to make those medic-alert bracelets?

Remember how much better nostalgia used to be?

I got a ticket for driving while talking on my cell phone. Is it worth arguing that I wasn't actually talking, just playing Tetris?

When I'm at the urinal, I always pour a little on the ground for my homies with urinary tract infections.

I'd take your message of social upheaval much more seriously if your "Anarchy" patch hadn't clearly been purchased at Hot Topic.

Women want a fairytale romance. Men just want a happy ending.

MAD'S LESS-THAN-MAGICAL OUTTAKES FROM Harry Potter AND THE DEATHLY HALLOWS

Don't **pee yourself…** don't pee yourself…**hold it** until you finish **fighting** the **Dark Lord…**Don't… **oh, damnit!**

What do you **mean** they cast **someone else** in the **Carrot Top** biopic?!?

For the **last** time, it's not a **muumuu,** it's a **smock!**

I **hate** walking through these woods **alone —** I'm always **afraid** I'll run into one of those **losers** from *Twilight!*

Ugh! Someone just **ate** booger-flavored jelly beans.

More often than not, he tries to barter for his half of the rent.

Damn, I just mass-emailed these Miley Cyrus upskirts to *your* contact list. If you'd remember to log out when you're done, this wouldn't happen, bro.

Are you sure, man? I mean, I can give you the money, but this thing is like a collector's item. Alls it needs is a little electrical work. And some lava.

He refers to *your* laptop as *our* laptop.

Oh, man— so *THAT'S* why my Honeycombs taste like pus sacks!

Ah, your first apartment: four walls, a couple couches... and a roommate passed out in his own filth. Let's face it, you're young and broke, so you'll have to get a roomie. And chances are he's going to be a total jerk — after all, he *did* agree to room with you! At least now you can tell for certain with these...

SIGNS BAD RO

His cold sore cream starts showing up on your milk spout.

His mom has a key.

Well, I guess *these* sheets will need laundering. I'll just leave this pie in the fridge.

BEERS

Dude, it's a *squirrel!*

I know, but I could tell he was hungry, plus it'll give that blindish guy I brought home something to play with!

He's a sucker for anything homeless.

168

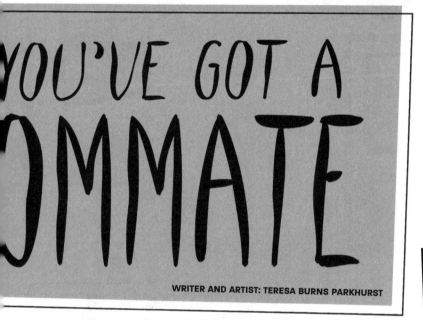

YOU'VE GOT A ROOMMATE

WRITER AND ARTIST: TERESA BURNS PARKHURST

Every few years, there are rumors of a gaming breakthrough — a hot new development that's going to revolutionize the way people play! But let's face it — those are just rumors. And most of the time, the "gaming breakthrough" turns out to be just another over-hyped waste of money that stinks worse than the inside of Master Chief's helmet. Still, the electronic rumor-mill was spinning particularly wild this past holiday season about the latest gizmo from Microsoft — the Zune! But since no one owns one of those techno-turkeys, we present instead…

WILD, UNFOUNDED RUMORS SURROUNDING THE XBOX KINECT

First time users often experience motion detection sickness.

A new rating system has been developed to gauge just how stupid you'll look when playing.

An unnecessary and highly-sensitive fart recognition system only serves to slow things down.

The exaggerated motions you need for racing games will eventually take a toll on your real-life driving ability.

WRITER AND ARTIST: JOHN CALDWELL

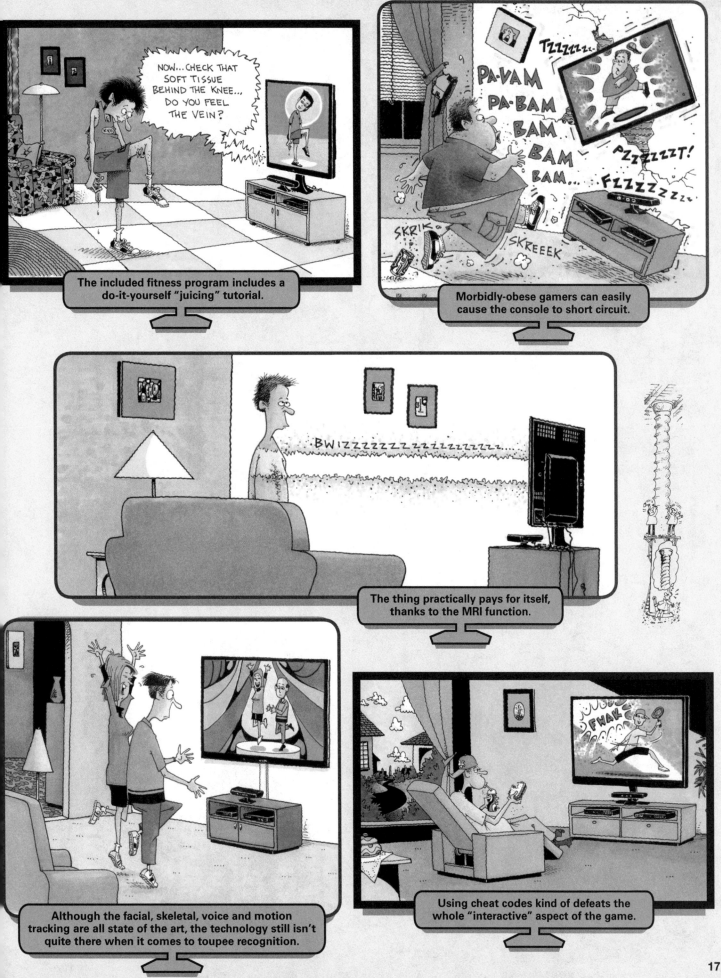

SERGIO ARAGONÉS Presents A MAD LOOK

WRITER AND ARTIST: SERGIO ARAGONÉS   COLORIST: TOM LUTH

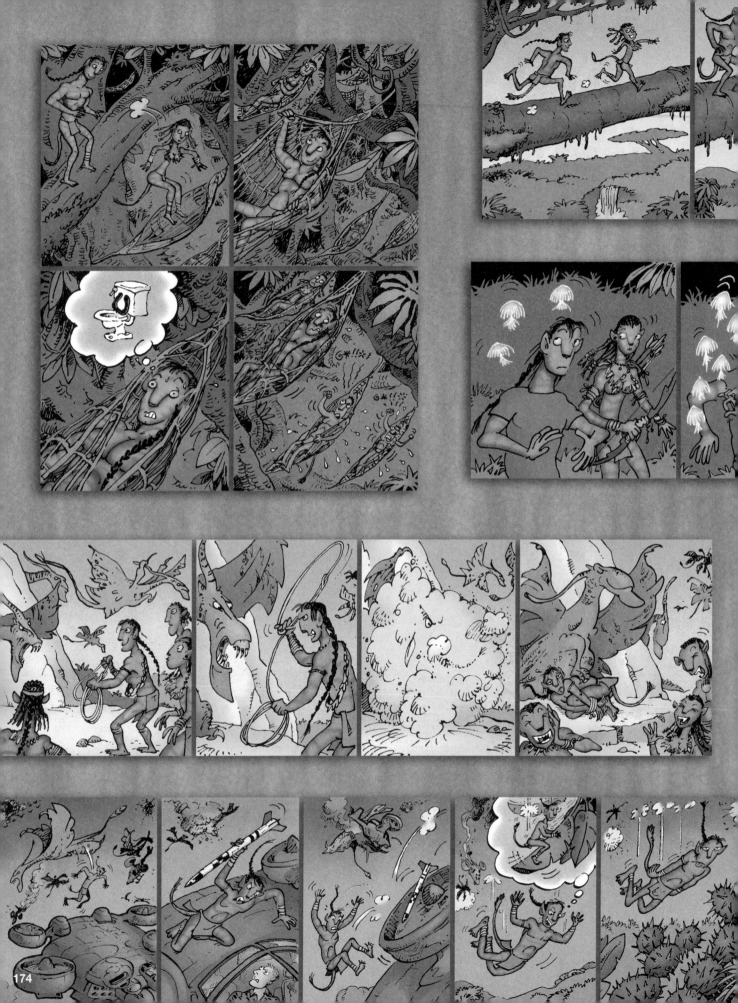

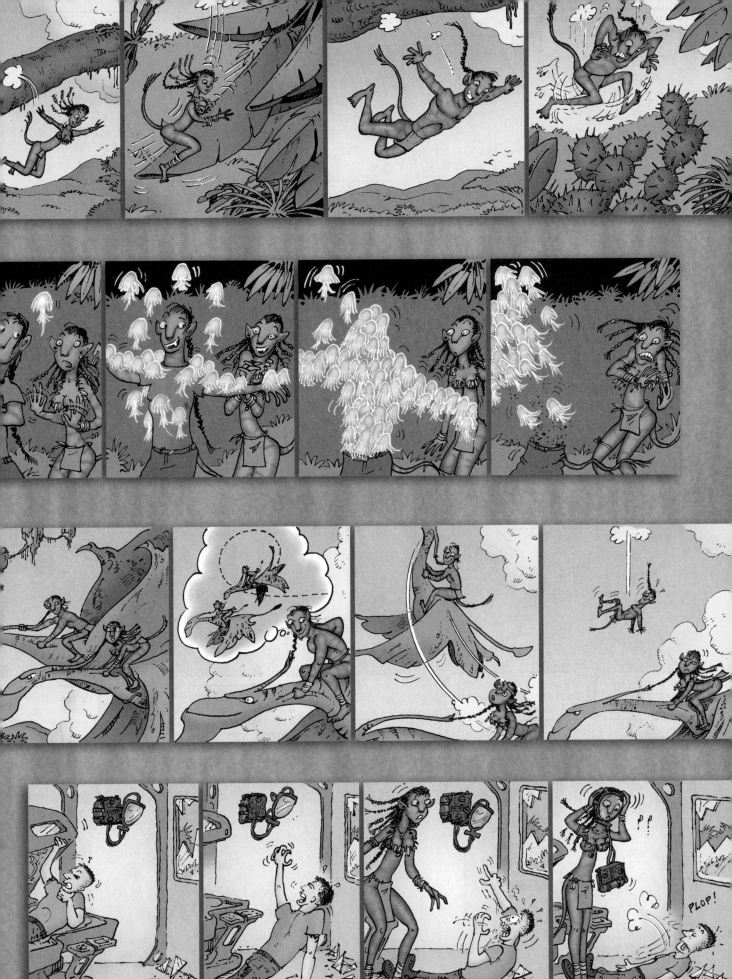

PLOP!

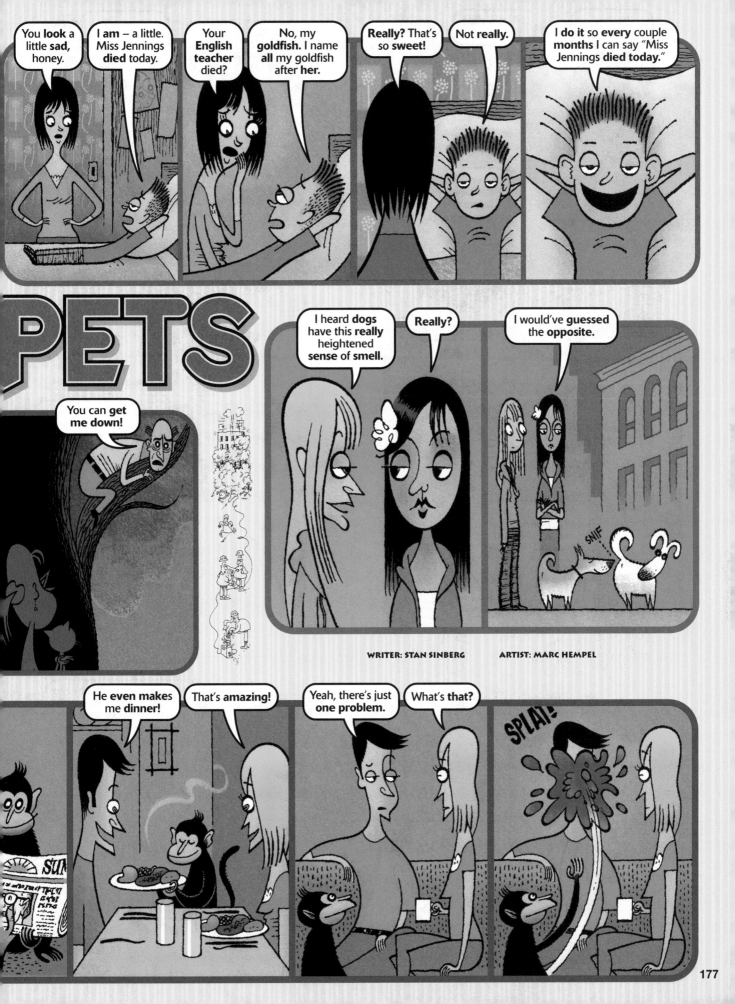

182

Sometimes it seems as if Hollywood doesn't make original movies any more, they just make sequels. Then, sequels to sequels. And don't even get us started on prequels! What's next? Well, if their streak of unoriginality continues, how long before the film industry starts combining hit movies in an effort to milk every last cent out of a franchise? Well, we here at MAD are also known for our lack of originality, so we're beating Tinseltown execs at their own game with the following two-pager called…

MOVIE

BLAIR WITCH project RUNWAY

STAR BOARDWALK EMPIRE STRIKES BACK WARS

THE LION KING'S SPEECH

Dirty

MASHUPS WE'D HATE TO SEE

BRIDGET JONES DIARY of a Wimpy Kid

ARTIST: SCOTT BRICHER

Harry Potter

JURASSIC PARK & RECREATION

M2BS
MEN IN BLACK SWAN

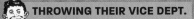

Scholars continually debate the existence of evil.
Pity they aren't subscribers to MAD. For, over the past few years, in the very
pages of this magazine, we've demonstrated beyond the shadow of a doubt evil's very real existence.
Beginning with priests, and then followed by clowns, carnival workers and countless others, we've vividly depicted
what happens when the darkness that resides in all men's souls manifests itself. Be afraid. Be very afraid…

WHEN VENTRILOQUISTS GO BAD

WRITER AND ARTIST:
JOHN CALDWELL

YICK! NICE GOING, CALZONE BREATH!

NOW LET'S TRY IT AGAIN WITHOUT THE TONGUE!

Sabotages C.P.R. demonstrations

HI, BOBBY! HOW ARE YOU —

YOU ⊙✦%☼☼ EATIN' PIECE OF ✂☼⊙ #☀☜ⅱ☜☝☜!

Makes the rounds at children's hospitals with his own
medically-challenged puppet "Little Toby Tourettes"

OH YES! LOOKIN' GOOD, MR. DOODLES!

NOW… JUST A LITTLE MORE OFF THE TOP!

FWIING! WUDDA WUDDA WUDDA…

Designing a new dummy always involves a visit
to a nearby old-growth endangered forest

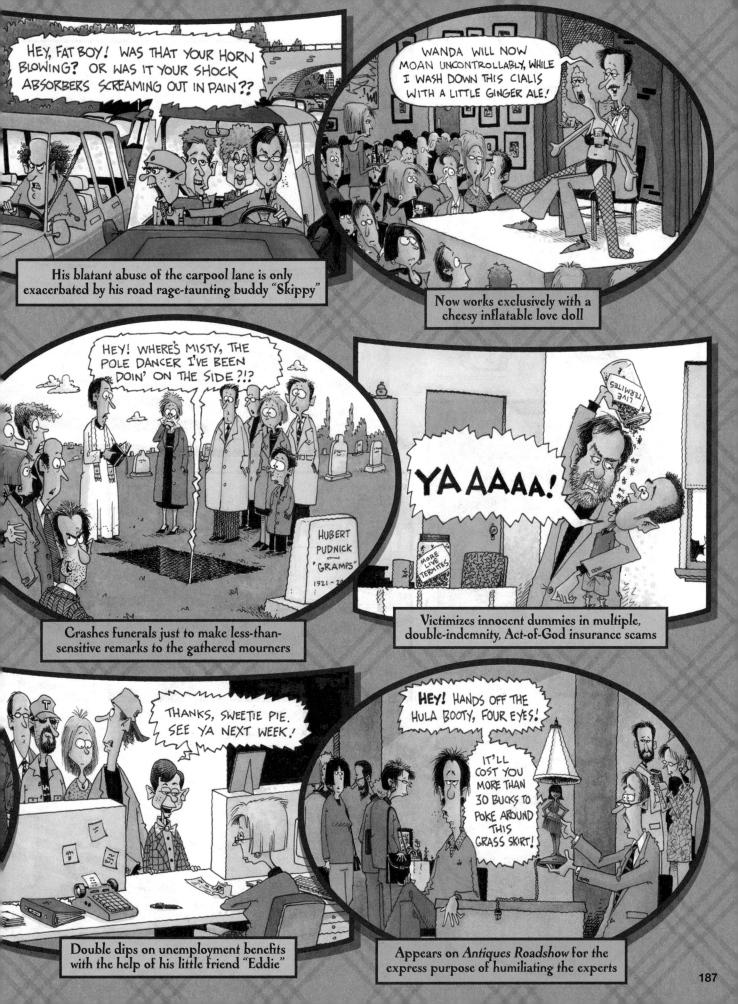

His blatant abuse of the carpool lane is only exacerbated by his road rage-taunting buddy "Skippy"

Now works exclusively with a cheesy inflatable love doll

Crashes funerals just to make less-than-sensitive remarks to the gathered mourners

Victimizes innocent dummies in multiple, double-indemnity, Act-of-God insurance scams

Double dips on unemployment benefits with the help of his little friend "Eddie"

Appears on *Antiques Roadshow* for the express purpose of humiliating the experts

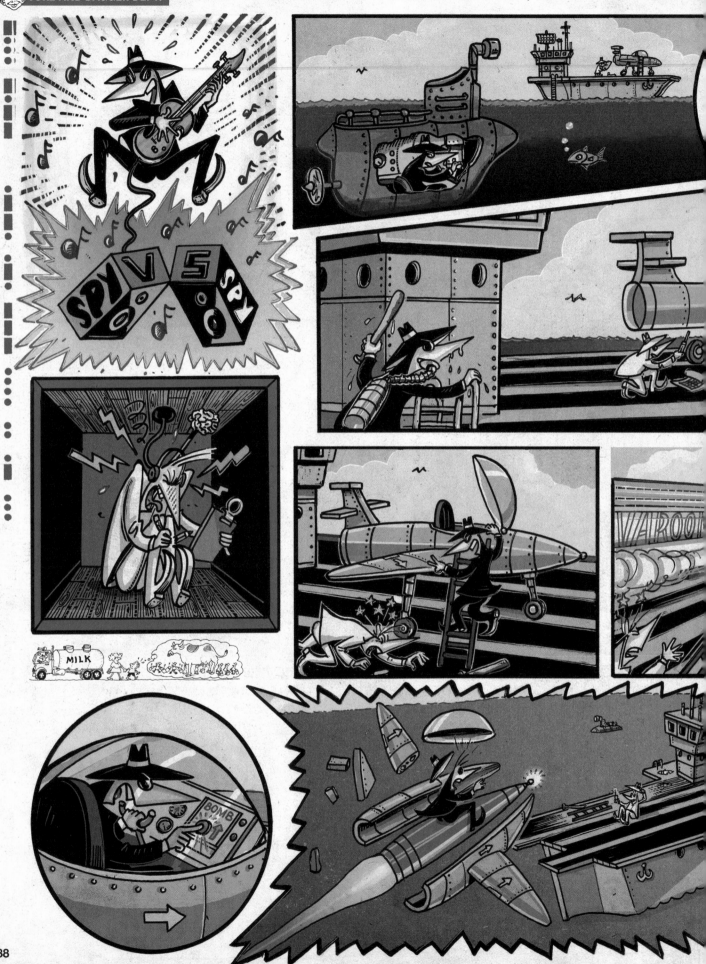

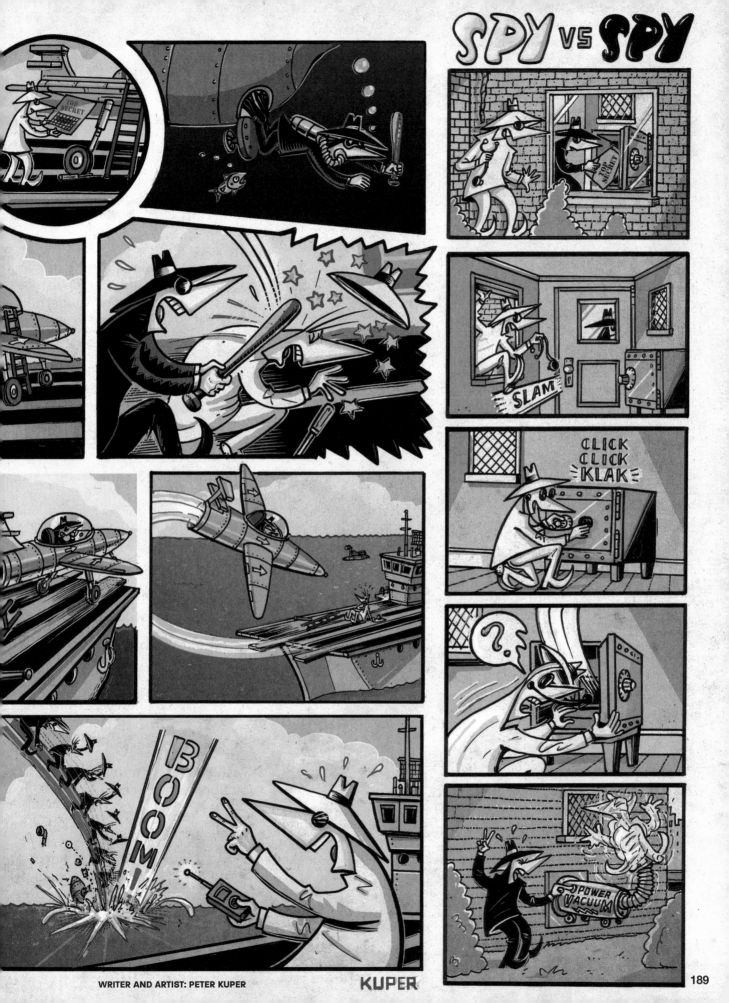

Twitter is tailor-made for self-obsessed, over-sharing, short attention span morons. And when it comes to self-obsessed, over-sharing, short attention span moron

KANYE WEST'S MOS

 Just brushed my teeth. Why don't they make Louis Vuitton toothpaste? And Gucci floss? I gotta make some phone calls
10:48 AM

 For my next album, I need a title as dope as My Beautiful Dark Twisted Fantasy. How about My Wonderful Crazy Backyard Koi Pond?
11:27 AM

My Sinfully Delicious Brown Betty Recipe?
11:28 AM

My Delightfully Eclectic Pound Puppy Collection?
11:29 AM

My Big Fat Greek Wedding?
11:30 AM

#Nowplaying Empire State of Mind by Jay-Z GREATEST SONG EVER
11:43 AM

 Big photo shoot tomorrow — gotta practice my dull stare
12:17 PM

Still starin
12:18 PM

Still starin
12:23 PM

I wish I dated a mermaid cause after you hook up you could eat her legs
12:59 PM

Just put on a fly-ass outfit: Viking horns, hockey jersey, yoga pants, alligator boots
1:36 PM

#Nowplaying Scenario by A Tribe Called Quest GREATEST SONG EVER
1:50 PM

T MORONIC TWEETS

Ever notice how hard it is to buy a decent albino rhino online? WTF??
2:22 PM

O WHAT if I got a $180,000 watch that has ny face made out of diamonds on it? Who DOESN'T have a watch like that? Hobos maybe
:45 PM

RUGULA SALAD WITH FENNEL VINAIGRETTE, ITCHES
:59 PM

Kanyelicious" not in dictionary???!!!!!!!
:24 PM

Nowplaying Blackbird by The Beatles GREATEST SONG EVER
:37 PM

The media's a bunch of bitches. Always wanting to build up the king so they can tear down the king. I don't need them lying-ass phonies
4:09 PM

Gotta remember to bring that up when I'm on MTV News, NPR and Regis & Kelly this week!
:10 PM

Nowplaying Crocodile Rock by Elton John GREATEST SONG EVER
:22 PM

People always sayin Kanye ain't street but AAAAAH! Lintball on my sweatervest!!
5:10 PM

Mila Kunis didn't get an Oscar nom?!? That **t is CRAZY!!! George Bush doesn't care bout Black Swan!!!!
:47 PM

Nobody wants to play Boggle with Kanye
:03 PM

FYI critics: I prefer "fascinatingly conflicted" to "comically unfocused"
6:15 PM

How come grasshoppers hate me?
7:17 PM

#Nowplaying All Night Long by Lionel Richie GREATEST SONG EVER
7:35 PM

I still have mad regrets about what happened with Taylor Swift. For one thing, I shoulda grabbed a boobie
8:52 PM

FOOTY PAJAMAS Y'ALL
10:57 PM

#Nowplaying Moon River by Clay Aiken GREATEST SONG EVER
11:02 PM

Hope I have my recurring dream where I'm the president of the USA who's also a sexy half unicorn that plays for the Lakers
12:18 AM

I got a new challenge for 50 Cent: see which one of us can tie the dopest Windsor knot
12:28 AM

#Nowplaying theme song from My Two Dads GREATEST SONG EVER
12:44 AM

Why don't hippos have wings? COME ON, HIPPOS
1:31 AM

Are you there, God? It's me, Kanye. Seriously, I've been texting you for like THREE DAYS WTF???
2:06 AM

WRITER: JACOB LAMBERT   ARTIST: SAM SISCO

The "Mindset List" was created by two professors at Beloit College in 1998 to reflect the worldview and cultural touchstones of entering first year college students. Recent lists have included the realizations that to those students (born in 1993), Bud Selig has always been the Commissioner of Major League Baseball and Czechoslovakia has never existed. At MAD, where there are no professors, we realized that from year to year, new college students were basically the same — but it was their cultural touchstones that kept getting weirder, as you'll see in our list of…

Disturbing Facts About The Incoming Freshman Class of 2015

1. They've never had to miss a phone call just because they were in a movie theater.

2. To them, Ellen DeGeneres has always been gay.

3. In their world, purple horseshoes have always been part of the Lucky Charms marshmallow lineup.

4. They've never played doctor with kids their own age, but they've texted pictures of their genitals to them.

5. To them, there have always been eight continents (including that enormous floating mass of plastic trash in the Pacific).

6. They've always been petrified of Catholic priests.

7. They've never had reason to complain that "MTV doesn't show music videos any more," because MTV has never shown music videos.

8. To them, The Star Wars saga has always included six films, three of them really crappy.

9. They've never had to churn their own butter. (Exception: University of Amish Fellowship freshmen.)

10. To them, the idea of actually paying for music has always been highly offensive.

11. They've never had to buy their porn from a magazine stand.

12. They've spent more time with grief counselors than guidance counselors

13. As far as they know, it's always been normal to develop breasts at age eight.

14. In their world, Lindsay Lohan, Miley Cyrus and Britney Spears are famous solely for being thoroughly screwed-up.

15. To them, the paternity of one's child has always been determined on Maury Povich's show.

16. Leaving their backpack unattended for 10 seconds has always been regarded as "suspicious behavior."

17. To them, MAD Magazine has never been funny.*

*also true of preceding 59 incoming freshman classes

WRITER: SCOTT MAIKO
PHOTO: JORGE SALCEDO/DREAMSTIME.COM